J B   C0275

VAM
Sullivan, George
    Phil   fighter
pilot.

EXTE

J B

VAM   C0275

Sullivan, George
    Philip Vampatella, fighter
pilot.

Ext. loan   Port Elizabeth   7/73

aug. 27/73 Wayne W Dilly

NOV 11/74*

DEC 23/75 Della Davis

5/10/76 James Haney

May 18/76 Scott McC

Dec. 21

This is an Authorized Biography

Philip Vampatella
FIGHTER PILOT

The complete life story of a college dropout who became
one of the first aircraft carrier pilots to fly over Vietnam

by George Sullivan

A RUTLEDGE BOOK
THOMAS NELSON & SONS
Edinburgh · New York · Toronto

To the pilots of the "tailhook Navy"

ACKNOWLEDGEMENTS

Scores of officers and enlisted men of the United States Navy were helpful in the preparation of this book. In particular the author wishes to acknowledge with gratitude the cooperation of: Cmdr. Sage Johnston, Service Information Officer, Naval Air Station, New York; Cmdr. F. S. Haak, Executive Officer, Lieut. H. T. Williams, Landing Signal Officer, and Ens. Dave Rosow, Public Information Officer, U.S.S. Forrestal; and Lt. Col. C. V. Glines, Magazine and Book Branch, Department of Defense.

The author is also grateful to the family and friends of Lieut. (j.g.) Philip Vampatella for their interest and cooperation.

PHOTO CREDITS

All photos courtesy of the U.S. Navy
except the following: Department of Defense, p 125
The Vampatella Family, pp 12, 16, 19, 22, 27, 34, 41
Rutgers—The State University, p 31; Armstrong Roberts, p 38

CONTENTS

chapter 1   SAFE ABOARD, *page 7*

chapter 2   THE GOLDEN BOY, *page 13*

chapter 3   ''WE'RE SORRY TO INFORM YOU...'', *page 23*

chapter 4   A NEW START, *page 35*

chapter 5   INDOC, *page 45*

chapter 6   SOLO FLIGHT, *page 59*

chapter 7   A PLANE CALLED CRUSADER, *page 77*

chapter 8   THE BIRDFARM, *page 87*

chapter 9   ASSIGNMENT WESTERN PACIFIC, *page 99*

chapter 10   INTO ACTION, *page 113*

chapter 11   THE HERO, *page 123*

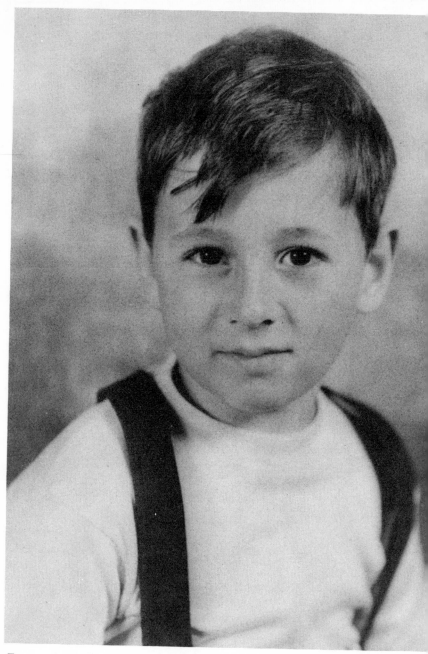

Future jet pilot: Phillip Vampatella when he was six years old

Chapter 1

Safe Aboard

Below, the aircraft carrier Lexington steamed, a thin strip of gray steel in the bright blue of the Gulf of Mexico. High above, Phil Vampatella brought his stubby, straight-winged T-28 jet trainer into the traffic pattern. He was tense but alert. He punched the button that lowered the landing gear. Then he turned the arresting gear handle to a "Hook Down" position.

Phil peered down at the historic "Lex" and at the thin white lines that outlined the landing strip. "Queen 6, Queen 6," his headphones suddenly called. "Descend to 600 feet. Begin final approach."

Phil eased the control stick ahead slightly. Quickly his plane responded and nosed into the proper angle of descent. At the same time, he rolled the aircraft out beyond the ship's wake and lined up with the straight white stripe centered on the carrier's angled deck.

The butterflies began to stir in his stomach now. They weren't unexpected. He knew his first carrier landing would start them fluttering.

Phil was used to rolling his plane to a stop over 6,000 feet on concrete runway. And he had done well in the simulated carrier landings he had practiced at the Naval Air Station at Pensacola. But this was different—a lot different. He was being asked to bring his plane down onto 300 feet of moving flight deck.

"Take it easy," his instructors had warned him. "Just fly the ball," they said. The "ball" or "meatball" they called it—the path of yellow light beamed up from the ship like a stream of water from a garden hose. Once on the glide path—"in the groove"—it was simply a matter of flying the beam down to the deck.

Once he had the meatball in view, he followed prescribed routine. He announced, "Queen 6 to Flight Control. Fuel, 1100 pounds. On meatball."

He concentrated on the thin beam of yellow light, oblivious to the roar of his jet's engine. The textbooks had made it sound easy. "Air speed, line up, meatball," is what they instructed. "If your air speed is right and your plane lined up with the centerline on the carrier deck, then all you have to do is follow the meatball home." A rugged year of study had gone before, and Phil could sum it up in three words, "Air speed, line up, meatball."

How well had he learned? In a minute he'd know.

Crucial test for a jet fighter pilot: first take-off and landing on an aircraft carrier, homing in on "meatball"

He wondered how it would feel when the plane's hook caught one of the stout arresting cables that lay taut across the flight deck. He was prepared for a stiff jolt, even though veteran pilots had told him not to worry about it. Yet he couldn't realize how his plane, traveling at better than 100 miles per hour, could be stopped in 200 feet without shocking him.

He was less than twenty seconds from touchdown. His altitude had dropped to 500 feet. He took another glance at the flight deck. It seemed to be rushing up toward him.

"If anything doesn't look, smell, sound or feel right, go around again," his instructors had told him. But to Phil everything seemed just perfect.

9

His hands moved carefully over the controls as he made last-second adjustments. He was cool and calm . . . and a bit surprised at his own confidence.

Suddenly the aircraft wrenched upward and out of the flight path. Phil gasped. Drops of perspiration trickled down his cheek. Just as suddenly, the plane resumed its normal course. What was it? Then he remembered. It was just "ramp burble"—the low pressure and slightly turbulent area that results from exhaust gases from the carrier's stack. His instructors had warned him about it and told him to pay it no mind. Next time he would be ready for it, but this time it was a shock.

Just ten seconds to go. Phil had the plane handling perfectly. His stick work was smooth all the way. There was no "throttle-jockeying."

Now the carrier's deck was just a few feet ahead. He knew he had to dangle the plane's hook well above the ramp, yet his angle of descent had to be such that 50 feet beyond the ramp the hook would catch one of the four arresting wires. If he got too high or if his angle of descent wasn't sharp enough, he would fly over the wires. He would "bolt," in other words, and would have to give the plane full throttle and come around again.

The plane roared over the ramp, touched down and held the centerline as if it were a train on a track. Phil felt the hook catch a wire and then bridle the hurtling aircraft to a stop. Phil was thrust forward in his shoulder harness—not enough to shake him up, but enough to let him know he had stopped.

Then a yellow-shirted deck crewman darted out in front of Phil's plane and gave him a thumb's up signal, so that Phil would lift the arresting hook to disengage it from the wire. Phil's face broke into a wide grin. The thumb signal told him that it was all over. His first carrier landing had been a success.

Phil let his plane roll aft slightly until he got the signal that the hook was free of the wire. Then, following signals from a deck officer, he taxied out of the landing area.

Aviation Cadet Philip Vampatella had passed his most important test. Behind him lay more than a year of Pre-flight and basic training. And before that, Phil could recall all too well, a period of terrifying failure.

Ahead lay six months of advanced schooling in the art of piloting a supersonic jet interceptor, and then assignment to an aircraft carrier operating close by a troubled land called South Vietnam.

Yet, through all that was to come, this was the day Phil would look back upon most often. Now he had in part justified the faith his family had always had in him. This was a day he had been aiming for, the day he became a fighter pilot in the "tailhook Navy."

Phil, three years old, the youngest in a family of six children

Chapter 2

The Golden Boy

Islip Terrace, on Long Island in New York State, is a small town—so small most maps don't show it. Its population has never gone beyond 2,000, and "downtown" is two dozen stores.

Though it is slightly less than 50 miles from the gaudiness and bustle of New York City's Times Square, Islip Terrace bears few marks of city influence. It is completely a residential community, and boasts neat one-story and split-level homes. Almost all of them have well-cared-for lawns. Huge trees—oaks, maples, elms—shade quiet streets. Illinois, Ohio, and Minnesota have towns like this. Any state does where the land runs flat and green.

Philip Victor Vampatella was born in Islip Terrace—in his family's home on Cedarhurst Street—on a cold morning in 1940. The date was March 31st.

"We'll name him after me," his father said. There was no disagreement. In Italian families the second son is often named after the father. In the naming of their first son, the Vampatellas had also followed custom. He was named Biagio (Benjamin), after the paternal grandfather.

"And for a middle name, I like 'Victor.' I think we should name him Philip Victor," said his father.

"Victor? Why Victor?" his mother asked.

"Well, I've always liked the name," answered his father. "And I have a feeling the name might help him to be a real victor, help him be successful in this life."

Philip Victor Vampatella's family was a large one. He was its youngest member. In addition to his brother Ben, who was then fourteen years old, there were four sisters, Angelina, Marie, Anna, and the youngest, Irene.

Philip's father had immigrated to the United States in 1912. Later he served in World War I. A few years after the armistice ending the war, he had purchased two strips of land on opposite sides of Cedarhurst Street and in 1930, not many years after he had married, he began to build the house that was to be the Vampatella home. He also built a small woodworking shop on the property. In addition to his work as a pattern maker and carpenter, he spent long hours learning to read and write English and, by doing so, he served to educate himself thoroughly in such subjects as literature and history.

His father's diligence made a deep impression on Philip as he was growing up. One day he confided to a sister, "If there is one man in the world I want to be like, that man is my dad."

The 1930s were not easy years for the Vampatella family. It was the time of the great economic depression in the United States and, like families everywhere, the Vampatellas had to struggle to make ends meet.

Yet it was consistently a happy family. Their mother saw to that. A short, thickset woman with a gentle nature and an unfailing good humor, Mrs. Vampatella raised her youngsters with large doses of love. Toward her, each of her children came to feel a great measure of affection and devotion.

Phil grew up with a deep regard for both his parents. In an autobiography prepared as an assignment during his high school senior year, Phil wrote: "Everyone at some time during his life makes the following statement, but I am really sincere when I say, 'My mom and dad are the greatest parents in the world.' "

The Vampatella household was seldom without the ring of laughter. Angelina and Ben were both blessed with fun-loving personalities. Marie, Phil recalls, could "pound out a lot of song" on the piano. Anna was regarded as the artist of the family. She could sketch and she had a talent for ceramics.

As the youngest child, Philip was deeply cherished by his mother. The whole family regarded him as someone very special.

"Mother never left him once until he was almost ten weeks old," Angelina recalls. "Then one night she wanted to see 'Gone With the Wind,' because everyone was talking about how good it was. She left me to stay with Phil and with instructions not to leave his bedroom. I didn't dare. Phil slept all the time she was gone and I sat beside his crib and stared down at him the whole time."

World War II was being fought as Phil grew up, but his memories of it are slight. Ben enlisted in the Navy, and Phil's father went to work for the Grum-

The Vampatella home on Cedarhurst Street, Islip Terrace, Long Island: It was a place rich in happy family memories

man Aircraft Company as an airplane pattern maker.

"I think my working at Grumman Aircraft served as Phil's introduction to aviation," Mr. Vampatella says. "He always had some interest in flying, and sometimes on Sunday afternoons we'd drive over to MacArthur Airfield to watch the planes land and take off."

But, Phil admits, as he grew up there were a great many other activities that interested him much more than flying. He enjoyed swimming and fishing in nearby Great South Bay off Long Island's south shore. He liked bike riding and he played Little League baseball. He mounted a basketball hoop in the backyard and it became an afternoon gathering place for neighborhood youngsters.

He worked, too. He had a newspaper route for a time, and often he caddied at Timber Point Golf Club, close by his home. One summer, when he was older, he helped on a bakery truck, delivering bread and pastry from door to door. He worked from six o'clock in the morning to two in the afternoon, and was paid fifteen dollars a week and, more important, all he could eat.

As a whole, life was comfortable for young Philip. His school studies offered Phil not the slightest problem, and when he graduated from grade school he was singled out to receive an American Legion "Good Citizen" award.

In the fall of 1954, he entered East Islip Union

Free School (now East Islip Junior High). His career there started on a jarring note. On his first day at school, upperclassmen forced him and his new classmates to walk barefoot about the school with their shoes in their pockets and their shirts on backwards.

A number of freshmen were embarrassed. "Why don't they leave us alone?" one complained.

"Don't worry," Phil said. "Next year it'll be our turn."

The next fall Phil spearheaded a group of sophomores that meted out similar indignities to incoming freshmen. However, Phil added some refinements, like sprinkling Tabasco sauce into the mouths of the new unfortunates.

Everything Phil did, he did with enthusiasm. He became vice-president of his freshman class. He tried out for basketball and became a member of the junior varsity.

Physically he was well suited for the sport. By the time he had reached his senior year, he stood just under 6 feet tall, and weighed a slim 160 pounds. He kept his black hair trimmed short.

All in all, his high school career was distinguished. He was president of the junior class and, in his last year at school, he served as vice-president of the G.O., the high school's "General Organization," or student governing body. He campaigned with the slogan: "P.V. for V.P."

High school in East Islip was a "breeze" for Phil, who was always an excellent, popular student, and a star athlete

Scholastically, Phil showed a consistently standout record. Math and the sciences were his best subjects and he could boast a report-card grade average of 90 per cent.

Not long before graduation, Phil received his greatest honor. His fellow members elected him president of his high school's branch of the National Honor Society. A nationwide organization of high school students, the society was formed and is supervised by the National Association of High School Principals. Outstanding students are selected for membership on the basis of their "achievement, scholarship, leadership, service and character."

Guided missiles was the field that Phil was thinking of entering. "Are you sure that's what you want to do?" one of his faculty advisers asked him one day.

"I'm positive, Mr. Gaines," Phil replied. "My best subjects are math and science. The field should be a snap for me."

"I don't know about that, my boy," Mr. Gaines said. "But I do know you might be happier if you were working with and for people."

Phil's brow wrinkled. "I don't understand," he said.

"You give so much to the school and to your classmates, I should think you'd consider choosing a profession where you'd be serving people. Did you ever think of becoming a doctor or a lawyer?"

Phil laughed. "No, sir, I haven't. I don't think that's for me."

Mr. Gaines shrugged. "I think you should really give it some thought, Phil."

"I've already started writing letters to engineering schools," Phil continued. "Guided missiles it will be."

Phil was the kind of son who would make any parents proud. The Vampatellas had not been able to afford to send their oldest son to college. But in Phil's case it was going to be different.

Phil's father had kept close track of his son's progress. "Don't worry about college," he told Phil early in his high school senior year. "We'll find a way to get you there."

"But it costs lots of money," Phil answered.

"I know. That just means we're all going to have to work a little harder. Your mother and I are very proud of you, and proud of your work in high school. We want you to be able to continue your education."

Phil smiled. "I know you do, Dad," he said softly. "But I worry about the money part of it."

His father looked up at the young son who towered over him. "Don't, Phil," he said. "We're going to build a house."

"A house? What do you mean?"

His father's eyes had a sparkle in them now. "You know the empty lot across the street?" Phil nodded.

"Well, you, your brother Ben and myself are going to build a house there this coming summer. When the house is built we'll sell it, and the profit we'll put toward college for you."

Through the summer the Vampatellas worked on the construction of a handsome brick house. By fall it had been sold, according to the plan.

Acceptance by a college had not been a problem for Phil. He had applied to several and was accepted by both Syracuse University and Rutgers, the State University of New Jersey. He chose Rutgers because of the fine courses it offered in engineering.

On the sunny September morning that Phil left for the Rutgers campus in New Brunswick, New Jersey, his world seemed without a problem. The road ahead loomed bright—without a hint of tragedy.

Phil, Mrs. Vampatella, and Phil's youngest sister, Irene, at home

Chapter 3

"We're Sorry to Inform You..."

Phil sat staring at the small clock on his cluttered desk. It was just past two A.M. He had been studying since late afternoon.

He rose, stretched, walked across the room and threw open the window.

He stood facing the open window, his hands thrust deep in his pockets. "And I said college was going to be a snap," he thought.

A shout from in back of him interrupted his reverie. "Hey! Are you crazy? Are you trying to freeze me out or something?" It was his roommate, Bob Wright, protesting from the top bunk.

"Relax," Phil answered. "I'm just getting a breath of fresh air."

"Fresh air is fine," Bob said. "But keep in mind it's January, not August."

Phil took a last deep breath and then closed the window. "Fresh air or not, I don't think I can stay awake any longer."

His roommate glanced down at the clock. "Holy cow! It's after two o'clock. You'd better hit the sack. If you don't know physics now, you're never going to."

"I guess you're right," Phil said. "But I really don't feel confident about that exam tomorrow."

"Who does?" his roommate asked. "But the best thing to do now is to get some sleep. That's what I'm going to do." And he put his ear to the pillow and shut his eyes.

Phil reluctantly gathered his notes together and closed his textbook. Then he snapped off the desk light, undressed, and climbed into his bunk.

Sleep didn't come easily. He was filled with anxiety. In high school, exams had never bothered him. Sometimes he did well without even cracking a book. Now it was different. Tomorrow's test in physics, one of his best high school subjects, had him in an anxious state.

"I just don't know enough to pass," he thought to himself. "I'm sure I don't." He tossed fitfully through what was left of the night.

The next day his fears were realized. The test bewildered him. "Sunlight falls on a divergent lens with a focal length of 20 centimeters. If a converging lens with a focal length of 20 centimeters is located 5 centimeters beyond this lens, where should a screen be placed to receive the sun's image?"

He read the question again. He read it a third time. "No use," he thought. "I'm not going to make it."

And he was right. Phil did fail his first semester of freshman physics. But he made up for it during the second half of the year. Meeting with his professor helped.

"You're trying to do too much," Professor Hoover had told him. "You're social director of your fraternity, and you're athletic director, too. You're running dances and scheduling basketball games. At the same time, you're trying to carry a full freshman schedule. You can't do it!"

"I guess I have to agree with you," Phil said. "It's no cinch here."

"You're going to have to make up your mind to spend more time on study," Professor Hoover said. "You've got the ability. You just have to cut down on your social life."

Phil took the advice to heart. The next semester he was the perfect student. At the end of his freshman year he passed every subject with flying colors.

He spent an enjoyable summer. His brother Ben, a bricklayer, got Phil a job as a construction laborer. He worked hard—and when his working day was over, he played just as hard.

When his sophomore year began at Rutgers, he returned to school with his usual enthusiasm. He determined to do well and plunged diligently into his studies.

Phil's homework usually kept him on campus for the weekend, but one Saturday late in the fall he decided he would go home for a couple of days. His sister Angie picked him up at the railroad station. Phil immediately realized something was wrong.

As they drove home, Angie explained. "It's mother. She's not feeling well. She complains about pains in her stomach."

"Has she been to the doctor?" Phil asked.

Angie halted the car at a traffic light. "She went last week. The doctor told her it's nothing to worry about, but that she should have an operation—an 'exploratory' operation, he called it."

The car was moving again. It was a warm and bright day, and the roads were lined with autumn foliage. Phil didn't notice. What Angie had said stunned him. He had never known his mother to be sick.

After a time he said, "I guess you can't disagree with the doctor. I guess she should have the operation."

The operation was performed. The resulting news was worse than any of the Vampatellas had imagined. "We found a malignancy," the doctor said. "We don't give her much hope."

"Cancer!" The word itself gave a sickening shock.

Phil returned to school the next Monday, but his mother's illness weighed upon him, as it would throughout the school year. He called home daily to check on his mother's condition. He visited home whenever he could. At school he tried hard to study, but thoughts of his mother robbed him of his ability to apply himself.

"You're not going home again this weekend, are you?" his roommate asked.

Phil continued packing his suitcase. He didn't bother to answer. He simply nodded.

"But we've got that big math exam on Monday. When are you going to study?"

Phil's mother in 1958, before the illness that took her life; later, prostrated by her death, Phil left college

Phil shut the suitcase and reached for his coat. "I'm going to try to get back Sunday afternoon," he said. He started for the door.

"Hey, you're forgetting your books!" Bob said, spotting Phil's math text on the desk.

"I didn't forget them. I'm not taking them, that's all." He left without saying good-bye.

After Phil had left, a classmate stopped in the room. "Say, Bob, what's wrong with Phil?" he asked. "I passed him in the hall, and when I said hello to him, he didn't even answer."

"I know," Bob said. "He's been like that for the last couple of months, ever since his mother got sick. I hope he pulls out of it soon or he's going to be in trouble with his studies."

True to the doctor's prognosis, Phil's mother weakened steadily. A hospital bed had been set up for her at home. She could not leave it. She lay there day and night, her body racked with pain.

Christmas was without its usual joy, and the family almost feared to look ahead to the new year and what it would bring.

It was a day of spring when Irene called Phil at school. "You'd better come home, Phil," she said softly. "Come home right away."

"I'll take the next train," Phil assured her. He did, but it was too late. His mother was dead before he arrived home.

Phil cried throughout the night she died.

"What can we do for poor Phil?" his sister Angie asked.

"I don't know," said Marie. "I've tried to speak to him and offer him some comfort, but I can't seem to reach him. I don't think there's anything we can do."

After his mother's funeral, Phil returned to school. It was the time of year when sophomore exams were scheduled. The important tests seemed to mean little to Phil, and he did poorly on them.

When he returned to college the following fall, he had lost all enthusiasm for study. The downhill slide that had begun the semester before continued.

Phil became friendly with a young man named Tom Harris, with whom he now felt he had a good deal in common. Tom was about Phil's size, but lighter, with blond hair and clear blue eyes.

Phil had gotten to know Tom the previous semester. Both of them had done poorly on their sophomore finals, so poorly that both had been put on scholastic probation. Sometimes this bothered Phil, but Tom's attitude was different.

"I couldn't care less," was the way he expressed it. "If I get kicked out of school it won't be the first time."

Phil knew his friend's record well. Tom had flunked out of two prep schools and finally managed to graduate from a third. He had spent almost two years at U.C.L.A., but he had gotten credit for only one. He had come East when his father was transferred to New York.

Though Tom could often be irresponsible, Phil found him fun. If nothing else, he helped to turn away the periods of depression in which he now often found himself.

Social events occupied much of Phil's time during his junior college year. He became vice-president of his fraternity and much of his time was now given over to planning frat dances and parties.

"Let's go into New York City," Tom said one Sunday afternoon, as the school year was drawing to a close.

"I didn't get in until almost two o'clock this morning. Let's just get some sleep," Phil answered.

His roommate insisted. "Come on," he said. "I promise to have you back early so you can get your beauty sleep."

Reluctantly Phil agreed to go.

Tom "revved" up his sleek red sports car; Phil climbed in and together they were off. New York was about 75 miles away and it seemed to Phil that Tom was trying to make it in an hour.

"Where will we head?" Phil asked, once they had entered the Lincoln Tunnel.

"Let's try Greenwich Village," Tom answered. "I'll show you around."

"And I thought college would be easy!" Phil learned that the College of Engineering at Rutgers was far from easy

Indeed, Tom did show Phil around—it was almost three o'clock in the morning when Phil suggested coffee, bacon, and eggs might be in order.

As they walked back to where the car was parked, Tom said, "Let's take a shortcut back to campus."

"Lead the way," Phil told him.

"We'll take the ferryboat to Staten Island. Once we get to the other side of the Island we'll be only a short way from the campus."

"It's all right with me," Phil said. "Just as long as you know what you're doing."

The sky was a velvet black as the ferryboat nosed into the slip at Staten Island. Phil, dozing in the front seat, was jarred awake when Tom started the car and eased it off the boat. Then he found the highway he was looking for and sped off toward New Brunswick.

Phil looked at his watch. It was 5:15. Less than four hours to his first class. He knew it was a class he had to make. He had used up his quota of cuts—excused absences. One more cut and he would flunk the course.

He closed his eyes and again tried to sleep as Tom raced the car across Staten Island. "I'm going to stop for gas at the next station," Tom said finally. "We're running low."

Phil roused himself to look at the fuel indicator. Indeed, they were running low. The needle was pointing to "E." But, when they got to the next gasoline station, they found it closed. So was the one beyond that. Neither Tom nor Phil spoke as the car roared down the highway. The problem was clear, and words wouldn't solve it.

Then the inevitable happened. The car's engine coughed, then stopped. Phil felt a sickening feeling in the pit of his stomach.

It was 7:30 before they could get a passing motorist to summon help from a service station for them. And it was after eight o'clock before the station sent a mechanic in a pickup truck to their aid. By the time Phil got back to the campus, it was after ten.

Phil knew that he was certain to flunk the course. Why cram for finals, he thought—it would only be a waste of time. When he had turned in his last exam, he threw his clothes in his suitcase. "Aren't you going to wait and see what your marks are?" a friend asked.

Phil answered with a shrug, and took off for the bus station. Back home, he once again went to work as a construction laborer.

"There's a letter here for you," his father announced one day. "It's from college."

Phil took the envelope and opened it quickly. He had expected the news, but still it stunned him.

Dear Mr. Vampatella:

> We are sorry to inform you that your scholastic average at the College of Engineering, Rutgers University, is such that we cannot permit you to continue your studies. . . .

There was more. But the rest wasn't important. He read the first paragraph again. Then he slowly walked upstairs to his bedroom, shut the door, and flung himself face down on his bed.

The bedroom was stifling from the heat of the July sun. And as he lay there, perspiration ran down his face and mixed with the tears that had formed.

His father, his brother, his sisters—everyone had sacrificed so to put him into college. He had let them down. It could not be undone. How could he ever bring himself to tell them? In a way he was glad his mother wasn't alive to see him so disgraced.

What would he do now?

Phil and his father, the day before Phil left to become a Navy pil

Chapter 4

A New Start

"Come on, Vampatella. Let's get some mortar over here," Phil's construction foreman yelled.

Phil was at work on a new school in a town near Islip Terrace. It was his job to keep the tubs filled with mortar for the bricklayers.

"Be there in a minute," Phil answered.

He rolled the heavy wheelbarrow up to the empty mortar tub, shoveled it full, and then returned to the mixer for more concrete.

"What's the matter with you today, Vampatella?" the foreman wanted to know. "You're letting the bricklayers get way ahead of you. How come?"

Phil shrugged. He had no answer . . . but he knew what was wrong. It was September and, for the first September in his memory, he was not returning to school to begin a new year.

If things were bad at work, they were worse at home. His father's disappointment in him was obvious and their relationship was often marked by long periods of silence.

"I'd like you to help me move some shrubs this afternoon," Phil's father asked him one Saturday.

Phil, his arms and legs weary from his week with the construction crew, gave a curt reply. "I'm going out," he said.

"What do you mean 'out'?" his father wanted to know. "Do you have a date? Are you going out with friends?"

"Out. Just out," Phil answered abruptly. With that he turned and left the room and went upstairs.

His sister Irene was in her room. Phil entered.

"I don't know what's the matter with me," Phil said. "I just had an argument with Dad over nothing."

"I know. It's getting so no one can talk to you at all," Irene said. "You're so touchy."

"I need a change, Irene. I need to get away."

"I don't think that will solve anything." She hesitated, and then added: "What about going back to school? If you make up some credits, you can return to Rutgers next fall, can't you?"

"That's what they told me," Phil said slowly. "But I've made too much of a mess of college to go back."

"What about getting a job in New York City?"

"Let's face it, Irene. All I'm qualified to do is be

a construction laborer. Who's going to hire me?"

"What about going in the Army or Navy? Did you ever think of that?"

"I've thought of it," Phil said. "One of these days the Army will be calling me anyway. Maybe I'll look into it."

Not long after, Phil visited the Navy's recruiting office in Bay Shore, New York. What he heard sounded right up his alley.

"Don't be upset about what happened to you at college," the Recruiting Officer said. "I know the course. It's very demanding. And you completed two years of it successfully."

Phil brightened a bit. These were the first words of praise he had heard in months.

"With your two years of college you can qualify for our Naval Aviation Cadet program," the officer said. "Then later, after you've received your commission, you can compile the credits you need to get your college degree. The Navy is just as interested as you are in having you complete your college training."

To Phil, haunted by memories of his failure, it all sounded like too much to hope for.

The Recruiting Officer continued. "You can't beat the training you'll get as a Naval Aviation Cadet. The education you get is worth as much as $125,000. That's about what it costs the Navy to train you."

"How long does training last?" Phil asked.

Going from a potential college graduate to a day laborer,
Phil spent long hours working construction in his home town

"Well," the Recruiting Officer explained, "it begins with four months of Pre-flight at the Naval Air Station at Pensacola, Florida. This is strictly a ground school. You'll learn military etiquette and military formations and other subjects to prepare you for the commission you'll receive at the end of Advanced Training.

"At Pre-flight there's an emphasis on physical conditioning, too. Through fitness and survival programs, your strength and stamina will be built.

"Last, Pre-flight schools you in subjects like aviation science and navigation, so you'll be qualified to progress to the next phase of training."

"It doesn't sound like any picnic," Phil said.

"It's not," the Recruiting Officer replied. "It's rough; it's rugged. A lot of fellows are washed out of the program during Pre-flight.

"After Pre-flight you get to do some flying, and even solo. Not in a jet, of course, but in a T-34 trainer. This part of the program lasts two months."

Phil nodded. It sounded exciting.

"If you have qualified for jet training, you'll be sent on to Meridian, Mississippi, for schooling in jet-powered planes. And in the final phase of this course, you'll learn to make a carrier landing."

"How long does all this take?" Phil asked.

"The training program takes eighteen months. When it's over, you'll be commissioned as a Navy ensign and you'll be awarded your wings—the badge that marks you as a naval aviator. Not long after that, you'll be assigned to the fleet, to carrier duty.

"Of course, you may prefer some other branch of aviation. Perhaps you would rather train to be a navigator, or a bombardier, or an air-borne controller."

"No," Phil replied quickly. "I'd like to be a pilot. That's what I want to train for."

"Do you think you can qualify physically?" the recruiter asked him.

"I guess so," Phil answered. "There's nothing wrong with me that I know of."

"First of all, you have to be between the ages of eighteen and twenty-five."

"No problem," Phil said. "I'm twenty-two."

"You're not married, are you?"

"No." Phil smiled. "No, I'm not."

"Your height and weight look right to me," observed the Recruiting Officer. "How about you eyesight and your hearing?"

"No difficulties there either," Phil replied.

"Then give it some thought," said the officer. "Look over these brochures. If you decide you'd like to make a try at becoming a Naval Aviation Cadet, contact the Procurement Officer at Floyd Bennett Field in Brooklyn."

"What happens then?" Phil asked.

"They'll set up a physical examination for you. And there is also a written exam. It tests your general

With renewed confidence, Phil set himself for the Navy. It would be difficult, but there would be no turning back now

knowledge and your mechanical comprehension. It's not easy," he advised. "Almost half fail to pass.

"Finally, the Navy will check your background," he finished. "They will probably interview your former employers, your high school teachers and your friends."

Phil took the literature the Recruiting Officer gave him. From it he found out that during his training as an aviation cadet he'd be paid $171.60 a month, and that he'd be provided with food, lodging, uniforms and medical care. Compared to the budget he had been on at Rutgers University, he'd be able to live like a king.

He also learned that if he decided to make naval

aviation his lifelong career, the benefits would be extremely attractive. Phil figured he could be eligible for retirement when he was forty-two; if he had gotten to be a commander by that time, his retirement "pay" would be $438.15 a month for the rest of his life.

Phil talked it over with his father. He spoke to his sisters about it. They agreed that the program sounded ideal for him. Less than a week later, he contacted the Recruiting Officials at the Naval Air Station, Floyd Bennett Field.

Then began a period during which he was physically examined and mentally tested until he felt that the Navy knew more about him than he knew about himself. This lasted for several months. "The Navy has a big investment in the young men it picks for this program," a Navy officer told him. "They want to be sure they get the very best."

During the examinations, a Navy doctor detected that he had a deviated septum—a malformation of the bony partition that divided his nostrils. It was such a slight defect that Phil had never even known it existed. Yet Navy doctors judged it was serious enough to prevent him from being accepted. So Phil had minor surgery performed to correct the condition.

At last, from Washington came the letter that notified him he had been accepted for training as a Naval Aviation Cadet. Report to Pensacola Naval Air Station for Pre-flight training, the letter ordered.

Shortly after, Phil, along with a small group of other recruits, was sworn in. The ceremony was held at Floyd Bennett Field.

He stood erect, his right hand raised, and repeated the solemn oath as it was recited by a Navy Commander.

"I, Philip Vampatella, solemnly swear that I will bear true faith . . . to the United States of America against all enemies . . . and that I will obey the orders of the President of the United States and the orders of the officers appointed over me . . . so help me God."

There was a brief pause. Then the officer said, "You are now members of the United States Navy," and he shook hands with the new recruits. Phil knew he was on his way; there could be no turning back now.

A week later, on a hot summer morning in August, Phil boarded a four-engined jet plane at New York City's LaGuardia Field for the flight to Pensacola, Florida, and the beginning of his new career.

As the huge plane roared down the runway and climbed above the layers of heat and haze over New York, Phil peered down. In a brief instant they left the city behind to head south, high above the blue waters of the Atlantic.

Phil couldn't help but hope he was leaving much of the past behind, too. Something deep inside him told him he was on the right track again. He hoped that something was right.

Drill sergeant greeting: "We're going to take the roundness off you..."

Chapter 5

Indoc

"Indoc" is what the Navy calls the period of Aviation Cadet indoctrination at the Naval Air Station, Pensacola, Florida. Cadets call it the "shock treatment."

In Indoc, the Navy telescopes its standard twelve weeks of basic or "boot" training into fourteen days. Khaki-clad Marine drill sergeants are in charge. It's rough and rugged.

When Phil arrived at Pensacola, he was assigned to a group of fifty trainees, almost all of them brand new Navy men, just as Phil was. They assembled in front of a two-story brick building, with huge white columns, that was pointed out to them as Indoc headquarters. A Marine sergeant addressed them. "We're going to take the roundness off you frat rats," he said, "and square you away!"

He continued. "The training here is of three types, you'll find: academic, physical fitness-survival and military. We're going to begin with the military. Stand at attention!" he ordered.

The group snapped. Later Phil was to learn that standing at attention—at first, at least—was not a simple matter. It had to be done "the Navy way." He had to stand erect, his chest out and his stomach in. His heels had to be together, and his feet positioned at a 45 degree angle. His thumbs had to be on the seams of his trousers; his palms had to be facing inward and his fingers had to be slightly curled. Last, his eyes had to look straight ahead. For any variation he was penalized.

One fellow in the group had a set of golf clubs slung over his shoulder. "Ship those home," the sergeant told him. "You're going to have about as much use for those as you would a safari outfit."

The trainees were assigned to rooms in the Indoc headquarters, four students to a room. But rooms weren't called "rooms." Instead, they were called "compartments."

During the first few days, Phil and his classmates struggled to get used to Navy lingo. The floor was the "deck"; the ceiling was the "overhead." The door became a "hatch," the window a "port" and walls became known as "bulkheads."

The time of day was always told in terms of the

twenty-four-hour clock. Five o'clock A.M. was 0500—zero five-hundred. Nine o'clock in the morning was 0900—zero nine-hundred. After twelve o'clock noon, twelve was added to each hour—one o'clock was 1300 (thirteen-hundred); eight o'clock became 2000 (twenty-hundred).

Phil's group of trainees was made up of young men of many different backgrounds. Some, like Phil, had had two years of college. They would receive their commissions when they were designated naval aviators.

Some were AOC's—Aviation Officer Candidates—college graduates who would receive their commissions at the end of Pre-flight training. A few others had come from Fleet duty with the Navy.

The Indoc day began at 0500 with the shrill call of reveille. Almost every waking hour was taken up in the business of "processing." Each of the prospective aviators received complete medical and dental examinations, even more thorough than their pre-induction checks. They received their shots. "Watch out for the square needle," one cadet kidded Phil.

They were issued their "dog tags" and clothing, principally the gray-green loose fitting coveralls that were to be their official "uniform of the day." Everyone was measured for an officer's uniform, complete except for the gold ensign's band on the sleeve. That gold braid had to be earned.

Indoc was where each of the students became the not-so-proud possessor of a brand new GI haircut. It took just a minute to get one, and the only instrument used was a pair of clippers. No scissors were needed— and afterwards, no comb. "Skinhead!" the cadets called one another.

Great emphasis was placed on discipline. Any trainee who felt his Navy schooling was going to be conducted in a country club atmosphere soon had his idea changed. Classes marched in formation to and from the classroom building—the "puzzle factory"— and the "chow hall."

Phil soon learned there was a right way and a wrong way to do everything—even to enter a room. When calling upon his battalion officer, he followed a precise procedure.

He stood squarely in front of the door to the officer's room, and then knocked—"pounded the pine" —precisely three times.

"Naval Cadet Vampatella requests permission to enter," he called out.

"Permission granted," came back the answer.

Phil entered the room, walked smartly to the officer's desk and stood at attention. Not a muscle moved.

The officer examined him carefully. "All right, Mister," he said. "That's going to cost you five demerits. You're moving your eyeballs."

Demerits were meted out for the slightest infraction—for not having one's shoes shined, for not having one's clothing properly folded or properly "stowed" in one's locker, or for an "Irish pennant"—any dangling piece of string or thread.

Rooms were inspected daily and had to be in perfect order, and the cadets struggled to get them that way. Sometimes they overlooked what they thought to be unimportant details.

"Look at that tube of toothpaste," the cadet officer called out. Phil peered into the medicine cabinet. He could see nothing wrong.

"Can't you see?" the officer asked. "It's adrift. The cap should be resting against the port side of the cabinet. The brand name has to be face up."

Phil knew enough not to make a sound. And he hoped his face didn't betray his bewilderment.

"That's going to cost you five demerits," the cadet officer said.

Cadets with demerits were restricted to the base. But demerits could be worked off on the "grinder," a quarter acre of blacktopped parking lot. Here on Saturday afternoons cadet wrongdoers marched back and forth in tight formation under the hot Florida sun. An hour of marching absolved the cadet of five demerits.

The period of Indoc passed very swiftly. The days were so hectic that Phil had no time to dwell on the

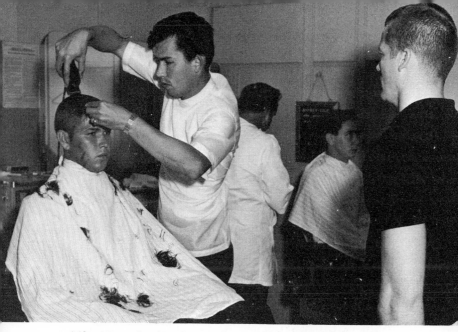

The Navy barbershop, where men received the sixty-second GI haircut; it was here that Phil was nicknamed "skinhead"

problems that had seemed so terribly serious just two weeks before. Islip Terrace, in fact, seemed a whole world apart from his new life.

After Indoc, the cadets moved on to Pre-flight training. In their first class, they learned that the emphasis was on "pre" and not on "flight."

"At Pensacola, the feel of the desk precedes the feel of the cockpit," their instructor told them. "Never forget that you men are going to be officers first and aviators second. You should regard your Pre-flight training as kind of an officers' training school, but one tailored for the aviation officer."

He continued. "There's a second reason, too, why you'll find an emphasis here on book work. It's because the Navy found out long ago that long hours of classroom study pay big dividends in the air."

As in Indoc, in Pre-flight the day began at 0530. The cadets started classes at 0700. At 1630—4:30 in the afternoon—classes were over for the day and the students were granted free time until 1800. In the evening, after dinner, there were two hours of supervised study. "Lights out" came at 2130.

The first week of classes was devoted to lessons in study skills, designed to teach the cadets the principles of rapid reading and comprehension.

Math and physics were the aviation sciences studied. There were also classes in navigation and engineering. The military phase of the training entailed military etiquette, formations and leadership.

"College was never like this," Phil said to his roommate, Bill Elliott, during an evening study period. Bill was about the same height as Phil, but heavier and darker and more serious looking.

Bill slammed his book shut. "You can say that again. At Stanford, I took twenty hours of courses a week. The Navy is giving us eight hours a day."

"My brain is weary," Phil said. "I don't think I can get another piece of knowledge into it."

"I know exactly how you feel," Bill replied. "There's so much to cover. I'm afraid to drop a pencil in class. While I'm reaching down to pick it up, I lose over a week's work."

Pre-flight training at Pensacola also stressed physical fitness and survival. Students were taught how to recognize the difference between dangerous vegetation and reptiles and harmless varieties.

Then each student was required to put into practice what he had learned, when the class was taken on a three-day survival trip. The men carried only essential equipment such as compasses, knives and maps. They packed along no food. They had to forage for what they ate.

A cadet who had been through the survival course told Phil, "It's a cinch—if you like broiled opossum."

The swimming survival program was particularly rigorous. In an Olympic-sized pool, students were taught to become proficient in the sidestroke, the backstroke, the breaststroke and the crawl. They had to learn how to "drownproof" themselves, to float and to breathe for unlimited periods of time.

The student aviators learned how to use different items of their clothing as an aid to survival. They learned to recover from the "Dilbert Dunker," in a simulated aircraft ditching exercise.

One upperclassman told Phil, "I've spent so much time in the water that I look like a prune."

Phil met his first real personal test during the course of swimming instruction. Each of the cadets had to be able to swim a full mile—completely clothed —in less than ninety minutes.

Phil could swim, but he had never swum a mile. And he had never swum a single foot with all his clothes on.

With a dozen other cadets, he plunged into the water from the pool deck and began circling. Despite the burden of his flight suit, the first half mile was easy. He completed it in just over half an hour. He could have made it in faster time, but he was carefully pacing himself.

Then he began to fall behind the schedule he had planned. From the pool deck, the supervisor shouted instructions. "You're slowing down, Vampatella. Get that crawl stroke going."

Phil wanted to answer, but he figured he'd better

Phil went through the twelve weeks of "boot" training in a fourteen-day period. It was rough and it was rugged

save his energy. He needed every bit of breath he could get.

He started to stroke again, but very slowly. His arms had grown weary and his shoulders ached. The muscles in his thighs throbbed painfully.

Scanning the surface of the pool, he counted eight swimmers remaining of the original twelve. The others had given up. Phil knew they would have to try again another day. They couldn't complete training without passing this test.

He swam another length of the pool. His eyes were beginning to smart from the chlorine in the water. "I think I'll call it a day," he said to himself. "I'll try again next week."

He had started for the ladder that led to the pool deck, when suddenly he heard the instructor shout, "Where do you think you're going, Vampatella? There's nothing wrong with you. Stay in the water!"

Phil did as he was told, but he didn't like it.

"Is he crazy?" thought Phil. "I can't stay in here. I'm beat. In another five minutes they'll have to come in and get me."

Despite his assorted tortures, he circled the pool another time. "Keep going! Keep going!" the instructor urged. Phil noticed that now there were only five others in the water.

His water-soaked flight suit seemed heavier with each stroke. He felt now as if he supported a block of granite on each shoulder. The pain was deep in his arms and legs, and the slightest movement was becoming agony.

"I've had it! I've had it!" he shouted to the instructor. "I want to come out!" Again he headed for the ladder.

The instructor looked down at Phil and shook his head. A look of deep disapproval clouded his face. "Okay, Vampatella," he snapped, "quit if you want."

Quit! The word struck him like a blow. He couldn't quit—not again! He'd show them—he'd keep going now until they had to fish him out.

He looked at the clock. Twenty minutes to go—but he was confident now. He knew he could do it.

When the instructor saw what Phil was doing, he encouraged him. "That's the way, Vampatella!" He shouted. "That's the way! Just three more times around!"

The pain in Phil's arms and legs seemed to diminish and his pace quickened. He made it—and with five full minutes to spare.

"Nice going!" the instructor said. "I thought you were going to quit, but you only stopped for gas!"

Phil laughed. Maybe his days of quitting were over, he thought.

Free time "ashore"—off the base—was called "liberty," and as the trainees progressed through Preflight, they found that the liberty situation improved steadily. Indoc students were not allowed ashore at all, but on their second Sunday at Pensacola, trainees who qualified academically—and weren't restricted to the base because of an accumulation of demerits—rated afternoon and evening liberty.

Weekend liberty was authorized after about the third week, but "the gate was closed" Monday through Thursday until the last week of the Pre-flight period.

Once granted liberty, most trainees headed for the beaches. Pensacola offered miles and miles of white, sandy shore. Many of the young men in Phil's battalion were from midwest areas of the country, and they had never seen an ocean before.

Phil's college training helped him, but only slightly. He studied harder than he ever had before.

"Come on, Phil!" Bill Elliott urged one Saturday afternoon. "A bunch of us are going down to the beach. Get your swim trunks!"

"No thanks," Phil said. "Not today."

It wasn't easy to stay and study in a hot dormitory room on a sunny Saturday afternoon. But Phil did—and more than once.

Finally, one day, Phil's class and more than one thousand other cadets in training stood in careful battalion formation on the green carpeted lawn of the Pensacola parade grounds in dress uniforms. After a few short speeches by the base administrative officers and a personnel inspection, the cadets in Phil's bat-

Phil found academic the roughest part of Navy "Indoc" at Pensacola. Here, a class in electronic navigational aids

talion were called forth one at a time to receive their Pre-flight graduation diplomas.

"Cadet Philip Vampatella," he heard his name called. He walked smartly to the dais. The base commander handed Phil his diploma, shook his hand, and congratulated him. "Thank you, sir," Phil replied, and gave a brisk salute.

"Over the first hurdle," Phil thought. He had been under such pressure the past four months he'd hardly had time to look either ahead or behind. Civilian life had, in fact, become nothing but a vague blur in his memory.

He smiled to himself. He was making progress again. The rolled white diploma he held was proof.

"X" marks successful mission, and a pilot-student team logs in

Chapter 6

Solo Flight

"In just another week you will all be flying, gentle-men," the instructor announced. "Not alone," he was quick to add, "but in a two-place instructional plane.

"You will each have eleven flights of dual instruc-tion. The twelfth flight will be a 'safe-for-solo' check and the thirteenth will be your solo flight."

This was the news the cadets had been waiting to hear since their enlistment, more than four months previous.

After they had completed Pre-flight training, Phil and his classmates were transferred to Saufley Field, Florida, just 8 miles to the northwest of Pensacola, for the "Primary" phase of Basic Training. At Saufley—at last—they would fly.

But before their first familiarization flight, there was another week to spend behind a desk. This one, however, was easy to take; the courses were far less abstract. They centered upon the plane in which each cadet was going to solo—the compact T-34 Mentor.

The cadets were introduced to the "cockpit familiarization trainer," an exact duplicate of the Mentor cockpit, with all the switches and dials and controls. The cockpit's only difference from a conventional one was that it never left the classroom.

They were briefed on flying safety and on the air traffic patterns they would be using in the Pensacola area. They were taught how to conduct a visual inspection of the plane. Then they were issued their flight suits and parachutes.

Then came the day when Phil, accompanied by his flight instructor, walked out onto the apron for his first hop. The two conducted a pre-flight check of the plane. They inspected flaps and aileron tabs, rudder and propeller—more than fifty items in all.

Then Phil climbed into the front cockpit and the instructor into the back, out of Phil's view. Together they checked out the cockpit controls, ending with the intercom system. When they had both had their headphones clamped in place, the instructor asked, "Can you read me, Vampatella?"

"Roger, sir," Phil answered.

It was up to Phil to start the engine. He had learned his lessons well in the cockpit familiarization trainer, and his hands moved quickly and surely over the buttons and switches. But this time there was a difference. The engine was real. It coughed and then settled into a deep and throaty roar. The propeller spun.

Then a crewman dashed in to remove the wheel chocks. The plane captain gave Phil a "thumbs-up" go ahead.

"Fine, Vampatella," the instructor declared over the intercom. "Now start your taxi."

Phil released the brakes and rolled the plane slowly down the taxi strip toward the entrance to the runway. He was "sloppy" with the rudder at first, and once veered the aircraft sharply to the left. But by the time he reached the narrow strip of blacktop that led to the runway, he was doing much better.

"I'll take it now," came the instructor's voice. "But you be sure to follow me on the controls."

He roared the engine up to 2,000 RPM's for an ignition check; then gave the plane full throttle for a few seconds before settling it down to "idle."

He turned the plane so it faced straight down the runway. He released the brakes and eased the throttle forward. Phil, his hand on the stick, felt it move slightly backward. Suddenly he realized that they were air-borne.

The instructor climbed the plane to 3,000 feet and began to circle the area, explaining to Phil the boundary points of this and all his future training flights. He pointed out a paper mill, the northern tip of Mobile Bay, and other "fix points" in the area.

"No other plane can fly into this area without permission," the instructor stated. "And we're not allowed to leave it."

Then the instructor showed Phil how easily the plane could be banked and turned. He put the aircraft into a climb and then a short dive. In his excitement Phil felt like shouting out, and might have if he hadn't been "wired" to the instructor on the intercom.

"You give it a try now," the instructor said. "She's all yours. Take it!'"

"Roger, sir," Phil reported. But he noticed his voice lacked authority.

Gingerly he eased the stick forward. The plane nosed downard, but only slightly. "Don't be worried," he heard the instructor say. "I'm still with you."

With that Phil thrust the stick forward decisively. The plane nosed over into a steep dive. "Easy does it! Easy does it!" the instructor called out.

Phil struggled with the stick to get the plane to level off. "You're over-controlling, Vampatella," said the instructor. "Remember, you've got an extremely responsive plane here. Whatever you want her to do, she'll do—and quickly. Relax! Take it easy."

Phil tried again, and this time he showed marked improvement. By the time the instructor asked him to turn back the controls, Phil had completed a couple of smooth turns and was feeling satisfied with himself.

Phil's instructional work in the T-34 continued daily. Even on days when it was rainy or overcast and Saufley was "socked in," the training went on, with the cadets practicing in the familiarization cockpit.

By the completion of his eleventh instructional flight, Phil had been trained in all phases of "air work," and in proper landing techniques and in the prevention of and the recovery from unusual flight situations like stalls and spins.

Then came his twelfth instructional flight, the pre-solo checkout, conducted by an instructor other than his own. Phil passed it successfully and was judged "safe-to-solo."

The next morning Phil's instructor turned the T-34

In order to qualify for aircraft carrier duty, Phil had to pilot the stubby T-28 trainer to a safe deck landing at sea

over to him. "She's all yours," he said. "Good luck!"

Phil had been trained well. He was cool and confident as he taxied to the runway. His takeoff went without a hitch. He climbed to 3,500 feet, leveled off and circled the field. Then he entered the traffic pattern and glided in for his landing. Gently he touched the main landing gear onto the runway and then the nose wheel. Perfect!

He taxied the plane back to where his instructor was waiting. He pulled to a stop, killed his engine, raised the canopy and then climbed out. As his feet touched the ground, he suddenly realized what he had done. He had soloed! His face broke into a wide grin.

His instructor grabbed his hand. "Congratulations!" he said. Several of his friends came over and pounded him on the back. Throughout his flight training, there were few days that thrilled Phil more.

Other cadets had soloed by this time. There were an increasing number of "air happy" trainees and some joyous celebrations at the base cadet club.

After they had soloed, the students moved ahead quickly as aviators. They learned stalls and spins and how to execute a split "S" and other acrobatic maneuvers.

As the eight weeks of Primary drew to a close, each cadet was asked to choose which "pipeline" he wanted to follow—jets or propeller-engine planes.

Phil had no doubts about it. He wanted jets. "As

long as I'm going to be a flier, I want to fly the fastest and the best," he reasoned.

After completion of schooling at Saufley Field, Phil and the other cadets were "transitioned" to jet flight training. For the next twenty weeks they were to be based at McCann Field near Meridian, Mississippi.

"Gentlemen," their instructor in engineering announced one morning, "this is a jet engine." To the instructor's right was rigged a special training model of a jet airplane power plant. The model looked as if someone had taken a normal engine and cut it lengthwise down the center. All the parts were exposed.

"This is the J-60," the instructor went on, "the type of engine that powers the T-2A Buckeye, the plane you're all going to be flying very soon."

Then he explained the major parts of the engine. The nose section contained a combined starter-generator. Just to the rear of it was a part that looked like a wheel, but mounted on it were slightly curved blades called "vanes." This was the centrifugal compressor.

In back of that came the combustion chamber. And after that a second "wheel," similar to the first. This was the turbine. The last section of the engine was termed the tailpipe.

"Now, gentlemen," said the instructor, "I'm going to demonstrate to you how these parts work together to propel a plane through the air, and I'm going to do it with this toy balloon." He took the balloon, a long and narrow one, inflated it and then held it high over his head. When he released it, it careened through the air over the heads of the students for a few seconds, and then it fell to the floor at the rear of the room.

"Cadet Cannon," said the instructor to a classmate of Phil's, "what caused the balloon to act in that fashion?"

The cadet stood up next to his seat. "Well, sir, when you released the balloon, you allowed the air to escape. The escaping air pushed against the outside air and forced the balloon to be powered over our heads."

The instructor shook his head slowly. "Mister, you have just failed the course in Jet Propulsion Theory and set naval aviation back by several years. What really happened was almost the opposite."

The instructor explained. "Recall that I forced air into the balloon under pressure, and when I released my hold on the balloon the air began to escape from the back."

He continued. "What this did was reduce the pressure at the opposite end. It was this difference in pressure that powered the balloon over your heads and to the back of the room."

Then the instructor explained the principle of the balloon's flight in terms of a jet engine.

"The compressor sucks in air through the air scoop in front," he said. "In the combustion chamber, fuel

As he brings the T-28 in for a landing, Phil lets down the hook, standard safety procedure to stop the plane short

is mixed with the compressed air. When this mixture is ignited, gasses are formed that expand to create terrific pressures. These pressures are so great they must escape or they will explode the engine."

"What happens to these gases, Cadet Cannon?"

"They escape through the tailpipe, sir," he answered.

"That's right," the instructor said. "You're reinstated. In escaping, the gases set up the same set of circumstances that existed in the air-filled balloon. At the front end of the engine there is a much greater pressure of gases than at the tailpipe end. This gives the forward thrust that pulls the aircraft through the air."

Jet flying introduced the cadets to the stratosphere,

that layer of air which begins approximately 7 miles above the earth. Flying in the stratosphere was going to produce problems they hadn't experienced before.

Most important, at altitudes beginning at 10,000 feet, oxygen grows very thin, and the pilot needs an extra supply. Without it a pilot could suffer from "hypoxia."

At 10,000 feet, hypoxia occurs in the form of a headache or quick fatigue. At 15,000 feet the malady is much more serious. The pilot's vision is affected and so is his judgment.

Phil could recall the effects of hypoxia that he had experienced during instruction drills in the use of oxygen equipment. In groups of ten, Phil's class was then shown the proper use of the oxygen mask and its regulator while seated in a huge steel, air-tight cylinder called a pressure chamber. An operator outside the chamber regulated the "altitude."

To demonstrate the effects of hypoxia, air pressure in the cylinder was gradually increased to what it would be at 25,000 feet. Phil, without any mask, was told to recite the alphabet. "A ... B ... C ... D ... E," he began. He got as far as "M," he was told later. Quickly an instructor had clasped an oxygen mask over his face before he blacked out.

The supersonic speeds the cadets were soon to encounter also meant new problems. To cope with this speed, each of the cadets was issued a "G suit."

Their instructor explained the working principle of the suit. "It has a very simple purpose. It works to prevent you from blacking out when speeds get to be more than the human body can normally absorb."

He continued, "As soon as G forces—gravity forces—start to build, the suit's inner rubber sacks automatically inflate and by doing so apply pressure to the pilot's body to prevent his blood supply from draining from his brain."

Before the cadets flew in the T-2A jet trainer, they were also introduced to the Martin-Baker ejection seat, a cockpit seat that would literally explode the pilot out of the plane should he find it necessary to bail out. Since first used in 1946, the seat had helped to save more than one-thousand lives.

A test seat mounted on rails that towered 40 feet in the air served to school the cadets in the operation of the device. When it came his turn, Phil strapped himself into the seat just as he did in an aircraft cockpit, with both a lap belt and a shoulder harness. He pressed the back of his head against the back of the seat. Then he pushed a button that fired the explosive charge.

There was a loud boom, and the seat rifled upward like a rocket from a launcher. He had a feeling that he was headed for the moon, but that his stomach was going to remain on earth. At the top of the tower, however, the seat eased to a gentle stop. If it had been a real ejection, this would have been the point at which he jettisoned his seat and "hit the silk."

Each of the cadets was given familiarization flights in a cockpit copy of the T-2A before getting to pilot the plane itself. Next they were given instrument time under a hood—or, as they called it, "under the bag"—in the rear cockpit of a two-place T-2A.

Then came dual pilot and then solo hops in the Buckeye. They learned formation flying, beginning with two-plane rendezvous and later join-ups and crossovers. This was followed by four-plane formation flying and day and night navigation flights.

The pace was still intense. In addition to their flight training, there were classroom courses in aerology, communications, navigation and engineering. "The Navy has more classrooms than airplanes," one student remarked.

Flying itself came easy to Phil. His fine timing and coordination helped him as a pilot. He felt there was no thrill in the world that could compare with the feeling he got when he was in command of the great power and silent speed of a jet aircraft. After he had soloed the first time in a T-2A, he became more determined than ever to achieve success as a naval aviator.

Those who, like Phil, successfully completed the Meridian phase of training, were returned to Pensacola for schooling in air-to-air gunnery. This, too, was a demanding part of training, for pilots had to use a "squirrel cage" technique in making passes at the airborne target—a banner towed by a plane 12,000 feet above the Gulf of Mexico.

The squirrel cage method of attack dictates that four planes, all at speeds of well over 300 miles per hour, execute successive rotating turns in firing at the tow target. To maneuver one's aircraft into the proper firing position requires maximum airmanship.

Following gunnery school came carrier qualifications, the final phase of Basic Training. It was a brief period—less than three weeks—but a trying one. Hours were spent in the two-place Buckeye, with the instructor giving pointers on how to fly "low and slow," the accepted manner of coming aboard a carrier.

Next came ten solo flights devoted to simulated carrier landings. In each, the pilot brought his plane down on a landing strip designed to conform to the space limitations of a flight deck. Finally came the carrier landing aboard the famed "Blue Ghost" of World War II, the carrier Lexington.

His qualification as a carrier pilot marked the end of Phil's first year as a Naval Aviation Cadet. But his schooling was far from over. Ahead lay six months of Advanced Training.

Phil and other cadets who had specified that they had wanted to fly jet fighters or interceptors were now transferred to the Navy's Advanced Training Command at Corpus Christi, Texas. And from there they'd go to Chase Field, situated at nearby Beeville, Texas.

At Beeville, Phil flew "hotter" jets. His training began in the F-9 Cougar, a stubby jet that had won renown during the Korean War. From the Cougar, Phil moved up to the F-11 Tiger for final training.

To Phil, the most important aspect of Advanced Training was his introduction to supersonic flight. In concrete terms this meant he would be piloting his F-11 at speeds of more than 730 miles an hour.

Breaking the sound barrier for the first time held no real fears for Phil and the other trainees, but they found themselves looking forward to it, nevertheless, with some slight apprehension. After all, it was less than twenty years ago that the sound "barrier" was

Before each flight, Navy student pilots give their planes a complete check. Here landing gear is given close scrutiny

looked upon by all as something very real indeed.

World War II planes like the F-38, P-47 or the F-51 that approached Mach 1—the term used to describe the speed of sound—often would hurtle out of control. The pilot would have to struggle furiously with his controls to check his plane's wildness. But there was no such problem with the F-11. She was aerodynamically designed for Mach-1 plus speeds.

"One look at the plane and you knew she was something special," Phil recalls. "Her thin, high-mounted, swept-back wing, and her overall sleekness gave her the appearance of tremendous speeds."

More important than any other was the "afterburner" feature of the F-11. When the pilot wanted a sudden burst of added power, he "cut in" the afterburner. By using hot exhaust gases to burn extra fuel, it gave the pilot all the additional "thrust" he could ever want.

The afterburner was used on take-offs and often in steep climbs. While it could increase a plane's thrust by as much as 50 per cent, it *doubled* the amount of fuel the engine burned. "Use the afterburner only when you are told to do so," one of Phil's instructors said, "or when it's absolutely necessary."

Finally, the day arrived when it was Phil's turn to become a Mach-buster. The plan was for Phil to take off in the F-11, climb to 25,000 feet, level off, cut in the afterburner and fire the plane through Mach 1.

At the time he planned to pierce the sound barrier, the plane would be over the Gulf of Mexico, away from homes and populated areas. On the ground the sonic boom sent up an ear-wrenching thunderclap. It could shatter a thousand windows.

After take-off, Phil put the aircraft in a steep climb. Even so the speed built. Phil kept a sharp eye on the Mach number indicator. He watched as the tiny needle nudged its way from 0.40 to 0.55 . . . 0.69 . . . 0.78.

Phil got set. He drew a deep breath.

Then he pushed the throttle forward and to the left, into the afterburner slot. The plane shot ahead. Phil was thrust hard against the back of his seat. He kept his left hand tight on the throttle. His eyes were glued to the small needle of the Mach indicator. It began to climb. It read 0.92, then 0.96. And then, Mach 1!

But the plane didn't ripple. There was no boom. There was no noise at all. Now the needle showed they had passed the speed of sound. They were at Mach 1.25—more than 800 miles an hour.

Phil came out of afterburner and then headed back to the base. He had passed another milestone.

In February, 1964, Phil's months of hustle and hard work were rewarded when he received his "Navy Wings of Gold."

"You worked hard; you deserve them," said the captain who pinned them on.

After flight in a T-2A Buckeye, student and pilot talk over achievement and failure on the way in to the check-in desk

The day had a double significance for Phil. At the same time, he received his commission as a Navy ensign. On receiving the commission, he swore this oath: "I, Philip Vampatella, do solemnly swear that I will support and defend the Constitution of the United States against all enemies, foreign and domestic; that I will bear true faith and allegiance to the same; and that I will obey the orders of the President of the United States and the orders of the officers appointed over me, according to the regulations and uniform code of military justice. So help me God."

Phil had his wings . . . and his next problem. That problem could be summed up in one word. The word was "Crusader."

Phil looks lost inside one of the squadron's powerful Crusaders

Chapter 7

A Plane Called Crusader

Phil never forgot his first brush with a Crusader. He was at the Naval Air Station at Meridian, Mississippi.

One afternoon the barracks were rocked by a tremendous roar. No one knew what it was. The whole place started to shake as if it were going to fall apart.

The cadets rushed outside. Streaking upward and quickly out of sight were a pair of mighty F-8 Crusaders. They had just taken off, and their flight pattern had brought them over the barracks.

"That really shook me up," said one cadet. "I thought they were coming right in the front door."

"I wouldn't want to fly those babies," another said. "I wouldn't know how to handle all that power."

Phil was inclined to agree. He knew that the Crusader was the hottest single-place plane the Navy offered. It was probably too much plane for one man, he thought.

Not long after the cadets began Advanced Training at Beeville, Texas, each was asked to fill out an "aircraft preference card." In this way the trainees indicated the type of plane each hoped he would fly once he was assigned to the Fleet. The Navy didn't promise that you would get the plane you wanted, but it almost always worked out that way.

The Navy offered a wide variety of aircraft, ranging from helicopters to supersonic jets.

But, of course, it was the jet planes that Phil favored. Some students wanted the two-man F-4 Phantom, the famed all-weather twin-jet interceptor and attack plane. Called "the best tactical fighter in the world," it had won fifteen world records for speed and altitude. In 1958, it had climbed right to the edge of space, recording 98,560 feet—19 miles—to establish a new altitude mark.

The Phantom could fly faster than 1,600 miles per hour—well over twice the speed of sound. Even the U.S. Air Force had no fighter to match it, and ordered the aircraft by the hundreds.

Another twin jet the cadets could specify was the A-3 Skywarrior, the backbone of the fleet's long-range striking power. Capable of flying 3,000 miles and more without a refueling stop, a carrier-based Skywarrior could carry out a strike against any target in the world.

Both the Phantom and the Skywarrior were operated by flight "teams." In addition to the pilot, there were two other specialists in the cockpit. One was a bombardier-navigator; the other was a radar-intercept operator, a man whose specialty was the interception of enemy aircraft by use of air-borne radar equipment.

However, single-place aircraft were preferred by the cadets, and first choice among these was the A-4 Skyhawk, a powerful attack aircraft. "It handles like a sleek sports car. It's real responsive and a pleasure to fly," a Skyhawk pilot told Phil. Other trainees had the same impression of the plane. Phil wrote down the Skyhawk as his preference over all other aircraft.

He knew that, although it was the world's smallest combat plane, it could carry a payload of conventional or nuclear weapons as big as that delivered by the giant B-17 of World War II fame.

The preference card asked for three choices. After the Skyhawk, Phil listed the Phantom. For third choice he put the Crusader.

Phil had talked to pilots who had flown the Crusader. He knew it could climb to 40,000 feet in just four minutes after take-off. It could fly faster than 1,100 miles per hour. Its top speed was a secret.

Phil remembered what one pilot had told him about the plane's afterburner feature. "When you cut in the afterburner, even at close to Mach-1 speeds, you get so much power the plane jumps ahead. You feel like you've gotten a kick in the seat of the pants."

For once, however, the Navy was not able to carry out Phil's desires. Late in his Advanced Training, he received orders that were to become effective when his schooling was complete. They informed him that he was to report to Miramar Naval Air Station near San Diego, California, and that he had been assigned to Squadron 211. And 211, Phil soon learned, flew Crusaders.

Phil shrugged. There was nothing he could do. The Navy needed Crusader pilots and they wanted him to become one. It was as simple as that.

At Miramar Phil saw Crusaders by the score. The long, slender fuselage made them easy to recognize.

After being brought into position by ship's huge elevator, a Crusader is wheeled into a hangar on the U.S.S. Forrestal

The plane looked exciting. Somehow, Phil thought, it looked mean, too.

Quickly he learned more about the aircraft. In addition to its four 20 mm. cannons, the Crusader could be armed with eight Zuni rockets or four of the remarkable Sidewinders, the heat-seeking missile that could literally ride up another jet's tailpipe and destroy it.

The Chance Vought aircraft manufacturing company had been given a development contract for the Crusader in May, 1953, after winning a design competition in which eight manufacturers had competed. The first production F-8 began reaching operational Navy squadrons in March, 1957. Each cost more than a million dollars.

In Vietnam the plane, though generally classed as a fighter-interceptor, was used to bomb and strafe enemy targets, and to provide protecting cover for ground operations or bombing planes. Another version of the Crusader was used in photo-reconnaissance work. And it was this plane that played so important a role in uncovering Russian missile sites in Cuba in 1963.

Soon after he arrived at Miramar, Phil began familiarization flights in the Crusader.

"How do you like it?" Phil's instructor asked him after his first flight.

Phil shook his head in mock bewilderment. "It's

just like the Coney Island roller coaster," he said. "All I did was hang on."

The instructor laughed. "I know what you mean. The first few times you just go along for the ride. But you'll get on to it. Don't worry."

Gradually Phil's ability to control the plane increased. He kept in mind what the instructor had told him. "What you have to do is think ahead of this plane; you have to be able to anticipate its every action."

Before long Phil had "carrier qualified" in the aircraft and became adept in the tactical use of its radar and navigation equipment. By mid-year he was judged "combat ready."

While the Crusader never ceased to be a demanding plane, Phil always found flying it to be a very rewarding experience.

When Phil was assigned to Fighter Squadron 211—nicknamed the "Checkmates"—he found flying a Crusader was to be only part of his responsibilities. He learned this during his first meeting with Commander King, the skipper of Fighter Squadron 211.

"We have 176 officers and men in the Checkmate Squadron," Commander King told Phil. "Each has a job to do."

The skipper pointed to a chart of Fighter Squadron 211 tacked to the bulletin board. On it were drawn rectangular boxes, each describing an area of

Phil flies the supersonic F-8 Crusader, mighty attack plane that adds punch to the offense of modern aircraft carriers

responsibility or a work assignment—a box for each person in the squadron. The descriptions ranged from Commander King's status as C.O. (Commanding Officer) to the scores of "ground pounders," the non-aviators of the squadron, mostly enlisted men, who were involved in the vital work of keeping the squadron's fourteen aircraft in operational readiness.

"Phil, as a pilot, you will have two jobs to do," Commander King continued. "You will be wearing two hats. You will have your flying missions, of course, but you will also have additional responsibilities within the squadron."

The skipper pointed to the chart. "Let's take an example: Lieutenant Cunningham is our squadron

Maintenance Officer. In addition to being a stick and throttle man (a pilot), it's his job to see that our birds (planes) are always ready to fly.

"Reporting to Lieutenant Cunningham are an Assistant Maintenance Officer and a Supply Officer and the various petty officers whose job it is to maintain the aircraft power plants, the various electronic systems and radar, the planes' ordnance, and so on." The skipper pointed to the corresponding box on the chart as he mentioned each job classification.

"Our Supply Officer was recently transferred, Phil, and we want you to take his place," the skipper said. "That means you'll be directly responsible to Lieutenant Cunningham. Get together with him as soon as possible to discuss what will be expected of you."

After his meeting with Lieutenant Cunningham, Phil wondered if he'd ever again have time to fly. "It's the job of the Supply Officer," Lieutenant Cunningham told him, "to maintain control over all the equipment and supplies the squadron requires."

Phil was introduced to the parts catalogs—enough of them to fill a 12-foot bookshelf. They listed every single piece of equipment the Crusader used down to the tiniest nut or bolt.

Phil learned that he was also charged with the responsibility of keeping a record of all the fuel and oil used by each plane of the squadron.

Next, Lieutenant Cunningham introduced Phil to

the seven storekeepers, enlisted men who would assist Phil in his new responsibilities. Last, he and Phil discussed the squadron's operating budgets. "Every piece of equipment you order, every drop of gasoline that's used, has to be charged against these budgets," Lieutenant Cunningham said. "Whenever you place an order, the information is fed into a computer. Periodically, our account gets checked. If our squadron is using more gasoline than it's supposed to, the Air Boss hears about it."

Lieutenant Cunningham continued. "If the Air Boss hears about it, the skipper hears about it. And if the skipper hears about it, I hear about it." A trace of firmness came into his voice. "If I hear about it, you'll hear about it." He paused. "Understand?"

Phil nodded. He understood, all right.

Checkmate Squadron was one of eight squadrons that made up Carrier Air Wing 21. The Wing was assigned to the Hancock, an aircraft carrier of the Oriskany class. Early in the summer of 1964, Phil and the other Checkmate pilots were ordered to report aboard.

What the future held was anybody's guess. The Hancock had been ordered to the Western Pacific with other ships of the Seventh Fleet. That covered a large piece of the world. It could mean Japan or Korea or Hong Kong or the Philippines—or Vietnam. They'd know soon.

The angled deck on the U.S.S. Forrestal allows more take-off room

Chapter 8

The Birdfarm

"Like steering Central Park from the top of the Empire State Building"—that's how the noted naval expert Hanson W. Baldwin describes the modern aircraft carrier.

The towering mast of the present day super-carrier rises about twenty-five stories above the four-acre flight deck. Other statistics are just as startling. A carrier like the Forrestal, or one of her six sister ships, is almost a football field wide and three full city blocks in length. From one end of the flight deck, golfer Arnold Palmer could drive with all his power and the ball would just about have speed enough to dribble off the opposite end.

Her giant turbines, connected to four five-blade propellers, can drive the modern carrier, at more than 30 knots, better than 700 miles a day. Her generators could light and power a city the size of Springfield, Massachusetts, or Grand Rapids, Michigan.

Never before has the world known a combat ship so large. She requires a crew of 4,500 men. This floating city has a chapel, a photo lab, a library, a clothing store, a bakery, a cobbler shop, a printing plant, its own radio and TV station, and three barber shops and three soda fountains. More than 13,500 meals are served each day aboard such vessels.

The first time Phil saw his carrier, the Hancock, she was tied to a huge concrete pier at North Island near San Diego. In reporting aboard, he strode up the gangway smartly, gave a crisp salute to the Officer of the Deck and presented his orders. The OOD read them carefully and then said, "Welcome aboard, Ensign." Then he told Phil how to find the Checkmate Ready Room, headquarters for the pilots aboard ship.

Once Phil found the Ready Room, the officer on duty introduced him to the pilot who was to be his roommate, a Lieutenant (j.g.) Hank Lawson. "Come on, Phil," he said, "I'll show you how to get to our compartment."

Into the heart of the ship they plunged. Phil followed and was led up a steep ladder and then through dimly lit passageways. It was easier for Hank, because he was smaller and shorter.

Phil looked at the room key he had been given. On it was imprinted: "03–106–4–1–L."

"What do all those numbers mean?" he asked.

"The first number is the deck," his roommate replied. "The hangar deck is the main deck and all levels above it and below it are numbered. The numbers above have a zero in front. They go 01, 02 and so on, up to 011. The numbers below the hangar deck are simply 1, 2, 3 and so on. You're on deck 03, three decks above the hangar deck."

"And the 106; I'll bet that's the frame number," Phil said. Hank nodded.

Phil remembered from Pre-flight training that frames formed the ribs of the ship's structure. They were placed about 4 feet apart and numbered in sequence from bow to stern. Like nameplates on mail boxes, small and shiny brass plates reported each frame's number. Since his room was located at frame 106, Phil figured he would be about amidships.

The rest of the key's code could have been written in Greek as far as Phil was concerned. But Hank explained: "The numeral 4 means the second space to port (to the left) from the ship's centerline. And the numeral one," his roommate continued, "is the first space to starboard; 2 is to port; 3 is to starboard; 4 is to port, and so on."

"All that leaves is the letter L," Phil said.

"That just means what the space is used for, L means 'Living Quarters,' " Hank replied.

Inside, the room was like a high-ceilinged steel

box. And everything in the room was steel—the two big wardrobes, the writing desks, the tiered bunks and even the sink was steel, the shining stainless kind. The room had been freshly painted a pale green except for the overhead, which was covered with a maze of pipes, ducts and conduits of every type and size.

Phil's bags had been shipped aboard ahead of him and now he started to unpack. "What time is the ship leaving tomorrow?" Phil wanted to know.

"At 0800 we're scheduled to be underway," Hank said.

"What do they have planned for us for tomorrow?"

Hank smiled. "Didn't you see the board in the Ready Room? They've got us down for a hop at 1300."

Air operations were in full swing early the next afternoon when Phil, fully briefed after a two hour session in the Ready Room, ascended a ladder to the flight deck. Some planes were being launched. Some, launched earlier in the day, were landing.

All about him was bedlam—organized bedlam, but bedlam nevertheless. The noise was intense. Loudest of all was the ear-piercing roar and whoosh of the jet planes as the catapult rifled them down the deck and into the air. Whenever a jet prepared for take-off, it set up a turbulent blast of hot air that stabbed Phil's nostrils with the acrid odor of kerosene.

Landing planes added to the commotion. As each

touched down on the steel flight deck, it sounded as if someone had dropped an automobile onto a sidewalk out of a ten-story building. After the plane's arresting hook grabbed a wire, steel arresting cables clattered across the deck. Once the plane had been stopped, its engine would rise in a high whine while the pilot taxied out of the landing area.

The noise of it all was so severe, the human voice could not be heard. For that reason, flight deck crewmen wore bright colored jerseys, the colors indicating the jobs they performed. Men who armed the planes —ordnance men—wore red. Fuelers wore purple; catapult men were dressed in green. The men who directed the taxiing of the planes on the flight deck

The tail hook on carrier planes is secret of safe landings. It catches, holds on steel cables stretched across the deck

wore yellow, and the men who pushed the planes about—called plane pushers—wore blue.

Work on the flight deck was terribly dangerous, Phil knew. There were constant hazards, such as being sucked into a jet intake, being blown over the side by a jet exhaust or struck down by a launching or landing aircraft. Men who worked on the flight deck received extra pay for their hazardous duty.

People aboard an aircraft carrier had a language all their own, Phil noticed. Planes operating from the ship were called "birds." And that made the carrier a "birdfarm" (not a flattop, the nickname used in World War II).

Phil and his fellow flying members of the crew were known as "airdales." The men who serviced and performed the maintenance work on the birds were "snipes." The name given to the enlisted men who operated the birdfarm was "blackshoes."

As Phil walked toward his plane, he noticed a pair of protecting "angels"—helicopters, or helos—hovering near the ship, one on the port side, one on the starboard. They were there to pluck pilots from the sea should one have to eject—"punch out"—from his plane. A "babysitter," a destroyer, trailed to the aft of the Hancock, ready to assist should search and rescue operations be necessary.

A pilot alongside Phil was speaking. "The Air Boss just told the driver of that A-4 that if he bolters again he'll have to leave the penalty box. He's in a low state," the pilot continued, "and if they don't trap him on the next go around, he'll have to take a drink from the whale."

Phil understood. What his buddy was saying was that the pilot (the driver) of an incoming Skyhawk (an A-4) had missed the arresting cables on the flight deck (he had boltered). Then he had thrust his throttle ahead and roared off the deck to come around again (went into the penalty box).

The problem was that the plane's fuel supply was dangerously low, and if the pilot boltered again he'd have to refuel from an air-borne tanker (a whale).

The maintenance of each aircraft was directed by a brown-shirted squadron member known as the plane captain. Phil spotted the captain of his bird, a big, smiling youngster. "How's everything this morning, Jimmy?"

"Everything is fine right here, sir," the young man answered. Then he pointed skyward. "But it looks like it might be a little rough upstairs."

Phil peered upward. The day was gray and over-cast, and Jimmy had merely confirmed what Phil had learned from the weather reports he had received in the Ready Room. The visibility was poor enough to use an instrument flight plan instead of a visual one.

It was almost half an hour before the steam sling-shot would power Phil and craft over the deck and into the air. Quickly he set up his pre-flight chores.

"Jimmy, look at this!" Phil called, peering up into a wheel well. "We've got a slight fluid leak here," and he pulled his fingers away to show his plane captain a black oil smear.

"I saw that earlier, sir," Jimmy said. "It's not serious. Just a worn gasket. We'll catch up with it as soon as you get back."

It wasn't anything to worry about, and Phil nodded his assent.

Then Phil scrutinized the general condition of the wings—the flaps, the leading edges, the formation lights and the access doors and panels. Last, he inspected the tail section.

Satisfied with what he had seen, Phil adjusted his helmet, clambered up the side of his plane and lowered himself into the cockpit.

Seated, he hooked into the one blue and one white leg-restraint lines that would force his knees together and prevent injury should he have to eject at high speed. Next he clicked tight the belt which clasped him firmly to the seat pan (and to a survival packet), and also the belt of the shoulder restraint harness, which pinned him to his ejection seat and parachute.

Then he plugged in his oxygen hose, threw the switch to the "on" position and clasped the green mask against his face. It was ten minutes to launch. Next he checked the instrument panel. Because he had done it so many times before, his eyes passed quickly over the array of gauges and switches. Each had to be at its proper setting:

Autopilot master switch: *off*
Landing gear handle: *wheels down*
Radio altimeter: *off*
Fuel dump switch: *off*
Fuel transfer switch: *off*
Master armament switch: *off*
Gun arming switch: *off*
Arresting gear handle: *hook up*
Engine anti-icing switch: *off*
Cockpit temperature knob: *as desired*
Instrument and console lights: *as desired*
Pitch trim knob: *neutral*
Roll trim knob: *neutral*

Once the panel check was completed, Phil signaled to Jimmy that he was ready to start the engine. He pointed the index finger of his right hand against the flat palm of his left hand, which he was holding vertically. Jimmy repeated the signal and then connected power from a small mobile starting engine into Phil's jet. With a powerful roar, the engine took life. Then Phil gave Jimmy the signal to disconnect the auxiliary power.

Jimmy stood in front of Phil's plane; he hugged his arms to his shoulders, and swept them straight out to his sides. This was the signal for Phil to spread

Thumbs up for successful landing on the U.S.S. Forrestal. The plane being caught by its hook is an A-3 Skywarrior

the plane's wings from their folded-up position.

Jimmy gave the signals for hook down and hook up and Phil responded by putting the equipment into operation. Jimmy ran through a score of pre-taxi signals and Phil answered each one. In this way, the ailerons, the pitch trim, the nose gear steering and the brakes and other working parts were examined for their operational readiness.

"One Zero One, Cat Two," Phil's headphones ordered suddenly. (Plane Number 101 taxi to Catapult Number 2.)

Jimmy and his mates removed the tiedowns that held Phil's plane secured to the deck. Phil let up on the brakes and they jockied him into position at the end of the catapult. Ahead Phil could see steam rising from the slotted catapult groove in the deck.

Once Phil was positioned over the "cat," green-shirted crewmen scurried beneath the plane and attached a short steel cable, known as a launch bridle, to it. Now the catapult officer signaled Phil to take tension on the bridle. He released the brakes and nose gear steering. The moment was at hand.

With his right hand he saluted the catapult officer. He peered straight down his take-off path, but out of the corner of his eye he could see the catapult officer bend down and press his thumb to the deck, the signal to fire the plane.

Phil started to count. Before he reached three, the catapult fired.

The plane thundered away almost like a bullet from a gun. In two-and-a-half seconds, Phil had reached the speed of 150 miles an hour.

He fought to keep his eyes open, but everything blurred in front of him. The G forces were great; he could not move an arm or leg. He could only sit motionless. Then he realized he was air-borne. The G forces subsided.

He eased the stick back and the Crusader climbed swiftly through the cloud cover and into the bright blue sky above. At 20,000 feet he leveled off and took a deep breath. He knew the turmoil and high excitement of a catapult launch!

Crusader gets a catapault launch: 150 mph in two-and-a-half seconds

Chapter 9

Assignment Western Pacific

Phil's days and nights were filled with activity as the Hancock headed west across the Pacific. Every day he flew at least one training mission, sometimes two. It was the same for every member of every squadron.

The routine was broken only by brief stopovers the carrier made at Pearl Harbor in Hawaii and, a few weeks later, at Yokosuka, Japan.

Then the ship steamed south to the Philippines and the Navy's base at Subic Bay, just north and west of Manila. After leaving Subic Bay, the Hancock headed west across the South China Sea. Everyone aboard knew what that meant: Vietnam.

In briefing sessions at the Naval Air Station at Miramar, and in the weeks that followed aboard the Hancock, Phil learned all about the country.

He had been so thoroughly briefed he felt he knew

Vietnam, geographically, at least, better than his native Long Island. He knew that North and South Vietnam combine to form a crescent-shaped strip of jungle and rugged mountain area that clings to the eastern rim of the peninsula of Southeast Asia. To the east of the country and to the south extends the South China Sea. The countries of Laos and Cambodia are to the west. China is to the north.

In total area, Vietnam is slightly smaller than California, but with a population of over 30 million it has more than twice as many people.

In 1940, the year Phil was born, the country of Vietnam, which was to come to have such an important bearing on his life, did not exist as we know it today. Instead, Vietnam and the two countries that neighbored it to the west had been joined to form a French possession known as French Indochina.

War is not a new phenomenon to the people of Vietnam. War, revolution and conquest have been known to that part of the world for thousands of years. Before the time of the birth of Christ, the Vietnamese had been conquered by the Chinese to the north, and China controlled the country for years. Eventually, the Chinese overlords were overthrown.

Vietnam did not hold its independence for very long. As Indochina it became extremely important in the French Empire. It boasted great agricultural wealth. The country was the third largest exporter of rice in the world. It also exported large quantities of rubber and corn. Deposits of coal, iron, phosphates and zinc added to its worth.

Indochina also could claim great strategic value. In addition to the border it shared with China, it had a common frontier with Siam. And whoever controlled the country was in easy striking distance of the Philippines, Indonesia, Malaya and Burma.

For these two reasons—for its agricultural riches and for its strategic importance—the Japanese put Indochina on their list of objectives. For five years, beginning in 1941, the Japanese held control of Indochina.

At the end of World War II, the French sought to return to Indochina, but the people no longer wanted French rule. Another eight years of bloodshed were set down in Vietnamese history.

In the years following World War II, a Communist government had come to power in China. It was filled with a desire to expand its rule and force its teachings upon the whole free world. Indochina was among the first of its goals.

Yet there were those among the Vietnamese who wanted no part of Communist rule, just as they wanted no part of French control. All they sought was the freedom to govern themselves.

In 1954, when the peace treaty that ended the war with France was drawn up, it sought to satisfy these different factions. It was agreed that country would be divided into two almost equal parts. North Vietnam was to be the domain of the Communists. South Vietnam was to be a non-Communist state, a free and independent government.

For a time the system worked well.

Then in 1959 South Vietnam was struck by two awesome problems. The existing government started to act like a dictatorship and free elections were halted. Many South Vietnamese grew dissatisfied and fearful of the future.

At the same time, the North Vietnamese went on the march. Bands of trained guerrilla fighters crossed into the South to join with pockets of Communist influence in a campaign designed to gain control of the whole country. (This enemy was called the Viet Cong.) The campaign was supported by supplies from Communist China.

In the fall of 1961, with the situation growing steadily worse, President Kennedy acted. In answer to a request from the South Vietnam government, the President sent American military advisers to help train Vietnamese units. This strategy had worked successfully in other countries when Communists had sought to rise to power. It had worked in Greece, in Malaya and in the Philippines. It worked in South Vietnam— but only for a time.

Late in 1963, the situation began to darken. The

government of South Vietnam was overthrown by a force of South Vietnamese military leaders. The Communist forces used to great advantage the months of turmoil that followed. Slowly they extended their control over much of the country.

They became increasingly vicious. In the first eight months of 1964, the Viet Cong assassinated 400 local officials in the South, and kidnapped another 700.

By early 1965, North Vietnam Communists were overrunning much of the country and American military strategy changed. A system of "enclaves" was developed. An enclave is similar to a beachhead, a coastal pocket carved out of enemy-held territory, and the scene of a huge military build-up.

Pre-flight checks are not limited only to equipment. Phil reviews target area maps for bombing mission over Vietnam

One day at a briefing session aboard the ship, a pilot said, "I still don't understand; what are we doing there?"

The briefer answered without hesitation. First, he recited history that demonstrated our country's deep concern with the countries of the western Pacific for many decades. He spoke of World War II and the Korean War, both fought in answer to enemy aggression.

"In Korea we learned an important lesson," the instructor said. "We learned that Communist aggression has to be met head on, as soon as it begins, or it has to be met later and in tougher circumstances."

Such were the events that led Phil Vampatella and his fellow Checkmates to be assigned aboard the carrier Hancock as she cruised her way west through the blue and calm waters of the South China Sea.

Once off the Vietnamese coast, they began flying missions. But these were simply reconnaissance or patrol. There was no bombing or strafing. The pilots attempted to spot enemy troop concentrations and report these to the South Vietnamese ground units.

American jet fighters had been used on only one occasion to bomb and strafe the enemy. In August, 1964, the destroyer Maddox had been attacked by enemy torpedo boats while the ship was operating in international waters in the Gulf of Tonkin, north and east of Vietnam. The American ship had answered the attack with its 5-inch guns. Then Crusader jets from the carrier Ticonderoga had joined in repulsing the assault. No American lives were lost, no damage done to the destroyer; the PT boats were left sinking.

Two days later the Maddox was attacked again, and so was a second destroyer, the G. Turner Joy. Again carrier planes helped turn away the attack.

The action angered our nation's leaders. President Johnson called it "open aggression on the high seas."

He ordered planes from the Ticonderoga and from the carrier Constellation, which had moved north from Hong Kong, to return like for like. The following day American aircraft bombed North Vietnamese naval bases, naval craft and oil storage depots.

After that raid, the skies were quiet over Vietnam for many months. Then in February, 1965, the situation changed drastically.

"Fighter Squadron 211, report to Ready Room! Fighter Squadron 211, report to Ready Room!" the ship's speaker blared. When the call came, Phil was asleep. The date was February 7. It was 5:30 A.M.

"Come on, let's go, Hank!" he cried, rousing his sleeping roommate. "Let's go!"

Quickly they washed, and then slipped into their dark-green nylon flight suits. By the time they arrived at the squadron Ready Room, most of the other pilots were already there.

The Ready Room always reminded Phil of a small

school classroom. The front wall was given over to a blackboard. Charts and maps lined the other walls. The chairs—there were sixteen of them—were heavily padded and they reclined like the seats in commercial airliners. It was in the Ready Room that the pilots spent most of their waking hours.

At the front of the room, mounted close to the overhead where everyone could see it, was a television set. Its screen showed only aircraft launchings and landings—nothing else. These were recorded on tape and "played back" through the day, so that pilots could observe how they handled their planes and thereby learn to correct mistakes.

At night or early in the morning before daybreak, the Ready Room was lighted in red. This was to reduce the difficulty pilots would have seeing once they were air-borne and in darkness. It gave an eerie glow to the scene.

Phil and his roommate took seats near the front of the room. Then Phil noticed that his name had not been listed on the flight board. Whatever the action was, he wasn't taking part; no doubt because he was a junior officer in the squadron.

Their skipper began to speak. "Gentlemen," he said in calm and even tones, "we've been ordered into action. Our assignment came less than an hour ago. It came directly from Washington.

"Yesterday," Commander King continued, "the

Viet Cong attacked our Army installation at Pleiku. They killed eight Americans. They injured one hundred others."

No one said a word. Coffee cups were set aside. The pilots scheduled to fly took out notebooks as Commander King began an explanation of their mission.

"Our targets this morning will be near Donghoi," the skipper said. He indicated the city on a wall map. Phil could see that it was about 50 miles north of the 17th parallel, the dividing line between North and South Vietnam.

"Donghoi is a major staging area for the North Vietnamese Communists. It's a starting point for the infiltration of men and supplies into the South."

Then the skipper held up a large reconnaissance photograph. "This is the city," he said pointing, "and this is our main target." He indicated a railway line that, on the photograph, appeared as a pair of white threads extending north and south through the city.

"I want you all to take a close look at this before you leave this morning," said Commander King, and he thumb-tacked the photograph to the bulletin board.

Next the Commander talked about radio frequencies they would use and about emergency procedures. "If you get in real trouble, head for the water," he told the pilots. Phil had heard that bit of advice many times before. Rescue at sea is much easier to accomplish than rescue on land.

Phil and a fellow pilot in flight suits, complete with the most advanced gear, designed for maximum safety in flight

"If you take a hit on the wing and start losing fuel, get hold of the tanker right away," the skipper cautioned. "Don't waste any time. And once you've made your pass, don't relax. They may not have any birds out, but you can expect heavy rifle fire and some machine gun fire. Keep up your guard until you're back on board ship."

Commander King never had a more attentive audience. His words, the pilots knew, meant success or failure, even life or death.

Then the Squadron Duty Officer, Lieutenant Dawson, informed them of the weather. "There are scattered clouds at 1,500," he told them. "It's overcast at 10,000. You'll have 4 miles of visibility."

Lieutenant Dawson also described the search and rescue planes and the surface craft available should an emergency arise. The pilots jotted the information in their notebooks.

"Other aircraft will be coming in before and after you," said Lieutenant Dawson. "Planes from the Ranger and Coral Sea will be in action, and so will Air Force jets from the air base near Danang."

When the announcements were over, the pilots set to work on their flight plans. They were calm and businesslike, yet there was a tenseness in the air. One or two cracked uneasy jokes, but the tension remained.

At 6:30 A.M. the six pilots of Fighter Squadron 211 assigned to the mission, weighed down by their G suits and other flight gear, filed out of the Ready Room to the escalator that would take them to the flight deck. Phil watched them leave. He was sorry he wasn't going.

Phil's turn came one morning two days later. PT boats had been sighted in the harbor south of Donghoi. Phil and another pilot had been ordered to "go and get them."

On the flight deck, Phil spotted the plane he was to pilot. He knew the squadron maintenance crew had worked through the night to have it ready. She was fully fueled and fully armed.

The sea and sky all around hummed with activity. Phil could see destroyers ready to protect against possible torpedo boat strikes and alert should a pilot have to ditch his plane. Helicopters were aloft, and so were fueling planes.

The air was filled with the piercing scream of jet engines. Phil set to work immediately on his pre-flight check. He gave special attention to the eight Zuni air-to-ground rockets that had been mounted in the Crusader's two launchers.

His pre-flight inspection complete, Phil climbed into the cockpit, saluted the cat officer, and was rocketed down the deck and into the air. Once airborne, Phil glanced below. The sea was alive with destroyers, cruisers, carriers.

At 10,000 feet, Phil rendezvoused with the other aircraft in the mission. Together they headed west toward Donghoi, a one-time provincial capital. He could see the crumbling French forts and the tin-roofed shacks and stucco huts of the villagers. To the west in the distance were jungle-green mountains. They were filled with Viet Cong guerrillas, Phil knew.

Then, in the harbor just below, Phil saw the reason for the mission—five torpedo boats. They looked small and harmless, but Phil knew they could cause the Hancock or any other ship mortal damage.

Phil adjusted the Zuni launching switch to a "ripple" position, so that he could fire two rockets almost simultaneously. He plunged his plane into a steep dive toward the blue harbor. At 1,500 feet he squeezed the trigger switch. Though his own speed was greater than the speed of sound, he saw the giant Zunis as they whooshed by his cockpit to streak toward the target, each like a bolt of armed vengeance.

After firing all their rockets, Phil and his squadron mate rendezvoused east of Donghoi for the flight home. Behind them they could see shattered and burning boats. There had been no anti-aircraft fire. Everything had gone as planned.

Once back aboard ship, they were debriefed. It was normal procedure for each pilot to describe his mission in detail. How many bombs and rockets had he delivered? Had there been any anti-aircraft fire? Were any enemy aircraft sighted?

Written reports had to be filed on the aircraft the pilot had flown. Were there any system failures? Was any corrective maintenance recommended? A complete review of the engine's performance had to be set down.

"Were you scared?" his roommate asked him later.

"Not exactly scared; but I sure was nervous."

"Were you nervous about the ground fire?" Hank asked.

"No; not that so much," Phil answered. "What bothered me was that I didn't want to make a mistake. I knew that the squadron commander was watching me, and so was the Air Boss, and the captain of the ship—everybody right up the line to Washington. I knew I just had to do things right."

Phil awaits take-off as crewmen ready his Crusader for the launch

Chapter 10

Into Action

"Any flak over the target?" Hank asked one day when Phil had returned to the room after a mission.

"Some," Phil said. "It looked like 37 mm. stuff."

Phil tossed his gear into a locker. Hank thought his roommate was strangely quiet.

"Everything all right?" he asked.

"A Skyhawk got hit." Phil said.

"Who was it? Is he O.K.?" Hank asked excitedly.

Phil sat on his bunk and lit a cigarette.

"I don't know who it was. I just know he was from the Hancock."

"How'd it happen?"

"I didn't see him take the hit, but some of the other pilots in his squadron did. They shouted, 'Eject! Eject! They've got you in the tail!'"

Phil continued. "But he didn't want to 'punch out'

over the jungle, so he headed for the ocean. Just as he got beyond the shoreline, his plane yawed sharply to the left. So he ejected right away."

Phil took a deep puff on the cigarette. "Because of the plane's angle, the pilot was shot out in an almost sideways direction instead of straight up. He barely had time to get his parachute open before he hit the water."

"Then what happened?" Hank asked.

"Viet Cong rifle fire from the beach began to hit all around him, so he started to swim away from the shore. Then other Skyhawks arrived. They made passes at the beach and stopped the rifle fire.

"His buddies from the squadron circled above him until Dumbo (a rescue plane) arrived. They took him aboard and flew him to the Air Force base at Danang."

Two days later the downed pilot was flown aboard the Hancock. He was in good shape except for a shin bone he banged up when he ejected. He was anxious to get flying.

The air raid on Donghoi was the beginning, and once begun the carrier air strikes continued with only occasional letup.

A few days after the first Donghoi mission, carrier interceptors, fighters and bombers, and land-based bombers, piloted by United States and South Vietnamese airmen, carried out a massive air attack against several military bases in North Vietnam. More than

150 planes took part. Three Navy aircraft were lost in the assault.

In the months that followed, air activity increased. Missions were ordered, not just in response to Viet Cong offensive activity, but, as one American official described it, "as part of our continual effort to resist aggression."

The Crusaders of Phil's squadron and from the Ranger and the Coral Sea, and Skyhawks, Skyraiders and Sky Warriors ranged over the entire country on an around-the-clock basis.

Air operations aboard an aircraft carrier after dark are unique to the conflict in Vietnam. They were judged too dangerous to attempt on a large scale during World War II or the Korean War. But modern science and technology have made nighttime carrier air strikes possible.

The launching of aircraft at night was never a great hazard, but recovery operations posed a problem. Nowadays planes come in for their landings at one minute intervals (not every thirty seconds, as in daylight). Pilots follow the meatball, the beam of light that dictates the plane's glide path. The angled deck is lined with white boundary lights, like an airport. In addition, white lights, flush to the deck, are set in the centerline.

Within the CCA (carrier control approach) room, radar tracks the incoming planes, and high-speed computers calculate the fuel that remains in each plane's tank. The air controllers know how many minutes each plane can remain in the air, and judge which planes must be brought in first.

"When you come aboard at night, you have to put your complete faith in the ball," pilots testify. Most admit a nighttime landing can be a "hairy" (scary) experience, and even the most experienced airmen confess it's never routine.

The types of missions varied widely. Phil and the other Checkmate pilots might be ordered to blast railroad bridges, river barges or truck convoys. They might be called upon to demolish a bridge, a strip of road or a railway line. Barracks and warehouses were often

Three Navy Crusaders fly formation over U.S.S. Forrestal, churning through the Pacific at a speed of over 20 knots

targets. There were reconnaissance missions to fly and, once in a while, planes—Skyraiders, particularly—conducted a "newspaper drop." This was a propaganda mission wherein tens of thousands of miniature newspapers giving our side of the war were dropped to the people in North Vietnamese towns and villages.

While the Crusaders would sometimes be called upon to stage a bombing or strafing mission, most often their assignment was "flak suppression." In this type of mission, Crusaders would be sent over the target area first, before the bombers, and attempt to knock out enemy gun emplacements so that the bombing planes could make their runs without the risk of anti-aircraft fire.

"Combat air patrol" was the second prime mission of the Crusaders. In this, the plane gave protective cover to bombing planes against possible attack from enemy aircraft.

With the step-up in air activity, Phil sometimes would have to fly two missions in a single day. This meant he would have to be in the squadron Ready Room for briefing at 0400. Soon after sunup he would be in the air. By mid-morning, mission completed, he would be back aboard the Hancock. By noon he was debriefed.

Then after a quick lunch the schedule would be repeated. He found there was never time for recreation and hardly ever time to write a letter home to his father or a sister. At night he would drop exhausted into his bunk.

United States air power over Vietnam was more extensive than that provided solely by carrier aircraft. Air Force light bombers—B-57s—and supersonic F-100s from air bases at Danang and Bienhoa lashed at the Viet Cong.

And from Guam, a small strip of coral and jungle in the Marianas Island group, 2,500 miles to the east, American military planners ordered into action huge eight-engined B-52 bombers of the Strategic Air Command. By later 1965, they were carrying out almost daily raids against Viet Cong "safe havens," transporting their bomb loads from Guam.

Each of the big jets was capable of carrying fifty 750-pound bombs. With such a payload, a fleet of B-52s could thoroughly saturate an area with bombs and, since they bombed by instrument, they could strike in any weather. Of course, for pinpoint accuracy, fighter-bombers like the Crusaders and Skyhawks were still the weapon most relied upon.

One day at a Ready Room briefing session, Commander King introduced an American news writer named Sydney Pace. "Mr. Pace has been assigned aboard the Hancock for two days," the skipper explained, "to gather information for the newspapers he represents in the United States. He'd like to interview some of you and I hope you'll cooperate with him."

One thing Mr. Pace asked about was the results the pilots felt they were achieving with their bombing and strafing missions. "What good is it doing?" he asked.

Phil fielded the question. "It *has* to be doing some good," he said. "I hear people say that the Viet Cong are moving their supplies at night. But when you fly over the country on a clear night, you don't see a thing moving. No people. No cars or trucks. Nothing. If they're moving supplies, they're carrying them through the jungles on their backs, and you don't move many supplies like that."

"Well, they're rebuilding the bridges and rail lines you fellows knock out, aren't they?" Mr. Pace asked. "So they must be moving some materials."

"We don't say we're stopping them," Hank chimed in. "All we claim is that we're slowing them down, and slowing them down a lot."

Mr. Pace jotted some notes. Then he had another question. "How do you know you're not killing innocent civilians when you bomb or strafe supply depots or truck convoys?"

Phil took this one. "We don't know, sir," he said evenly. "But we do know that everything possible is being done to prevent this from happening."

"That's right!" declared Hank Lawson. "Our air targets are based on reports of South Vietnamese intelligence agents. If they spot enemy troop concen-

Flying in a tight formation is learned by practice, with no second chances. Phil keeps his Crusader (106) in good line

trations, for instance, they report it to government headquarters. From there the word is passed to American military leaders."

"We try for pinpoint accuracy on our targets," Phil added. "Often when our bombers come in over a target they are directed by forward air controllers. They fly in low in single engine Cessnas and actually mark the targets where the bombs are to be dropped.

"Our job is to protect the South Vietnamese civilians," Phil went on. "That's what our military leaders have told us to do. That's what we're doing."

The newsman smiled. "You fellows don't sound like you have much of a morale problem," he said.

"Well, we try to do our job, sir," Phil said. "We

try to do what we're told to do. We realize that the President and the people high up in the Defense Department know a lot more about the situation here than we do. They make the decisions. We follow orders. That's the way it should be."

What the Navy, Marine and Air Force pilots have accomplished in Vietnam has not gone unrecognized. Air power, say qualified military experts, has done more to hurt the Viet Cong than any other single factor. Some sources state that the American bombing and strafing not only halted the growing strength of the Viet Cong, but actually saved the day during critical months early in 1965.

Late in the spring of 1965, the Hancock was ordered to return to the United States. The officers and crew were scheduled for rest—"peace, ease and re-freshment," one pilot called it. The ship itself was set for overhaul at the San Diego Naval Shipyard.

The carriers Ranger and Constellation also returned to ports on the West Coast of the United States at about the same time. Three other "floating islands"—the Independence, the Midway and the Oriskany—moved in as replacement vessels.

Day after day the Hancock steamed eastward until it seemed to Phil, anxious for a reunion with his family, that the Pacific was endless. Finally the verdant California coast loomed on the horizon. The men tingled with excitment; at last they were home.

Phil remembers being told: "If you get in trouble, head for the water"

Chapter 11

The Hero

Phil's courage in the skies over Vietnam had not gone unnoticed. He and the other members of his squadron were thrilled when they heard the news that they were each to receive the Air Medal, one of the highest awards the country can bestow for distinguished action.

The awarding of the medals took place on a clear, sun-drenched day after the Hancock had returned to San Diego. On the huge and open flight deck, the honored pilots stood at stiff attention.

The loudspeakers boomed the citation: "For meritorious achievement while participating in aerial flight."

"Meritorious achievement?" Phil could hardly believe they were talking about him. After all, he had only done what he had been told to do.

"Lieutenant (j.g.) Philip Vampatella," he heard his name called. And then Rear Admiral Edward Outlaw, Commander of Carrier Division One, was in front of him. A warm smile crinkled the admiral's ruddy features as he pinned the Air Medal to Phil's chest.

"Congratulations, Lieutenant," the admiral said. "It gives me great pleasure to make this presentation. With champions like you pilots in our line-up, I know we'll never go wrong."

Then he shook Phil's hand. Phil was so excited he could barely mumble, "Thank you, sir."

When the admiral moved on to the next pilot, Phil could feel his heart pounding. Even his first flight in a Crusader hadn't excited him this much.

Later in the privacy of his room Phil took a close look at the award. The medal was cast in the form of a compass and its face was a bronze disc. Across the disc an eagle in flight was pictured. In each claw the eagle carried a bolt of lightning.

Not long after the Hancock arrived in San Diego, the ship was put into drydock for a general overhaul. The pilots of Fighter Squadron 211 were assigned to the base at Miramar.

From Miramar, the Checkmates kept in professional trim with daily training flights. For a brief period the squadron was transferred to Fallon, Nevada, for gunnery and bombing practice. Everyone seemed to suspect the reason the squadron was being kept in combat readiness. Then one day the word came. The Hancock was soon to resume its duty station in the Western Pacific.

Before the ship left the United States, however, Phil received four weeks of leave time. When word was spread that he was returning to Islip Terrace, his friends and relatives filled the Vampatella home.

His father, in particular, wanted to know all about Phil's combat flights. "How many missions did you fly?" he asked. "Were you ever shot at? Were you ever hit?" The questions came thick and fast. Phil didn't know what to answer first.

He also wanted to know about Phil's plans for the

Phil took part in the mission over Vietnam, April 9, 1965, when his squadron attacked the Qui Vinh Railroad Bridge and the Phuong Can Highway Bridge. Both constructions were damaged enough to stop Viet Cong action on these routes

DESTROYED SPAN

ONE SPAN DROPPED

future. "Do you think you will stay in the Navy?" he asked.

"Well, the first thing I'd like to do after this tour of duty is over is get my college degree," Phil answered. Then he explained to his father the Navy's desire that he finish college.

"But I mean after that?" his father said.

Phil thought a minute. Then he said, "I'll keep flying the Navy's planes as long as they let me. Two weeks after I arrived at Pensacola for my Pre-flight training, I realized I wanted to be a Navy pilot more than anything else in the world. And I still feel the same way."

Then his father turned very serious. "We worry about you when you're in Vietnam, Phil. Do you mind going back?"

"I hope I don't sound corny," Phil answered. "But it's my job. I have an obligation. And I don't happen to be the only one that has this responsibility."

His father put his arm about Phil's shoulder. "We're so proud of you, Phil, so very proud," he said softly.

For an instant Phil's thoughts flashed over the events of the past three years and to the Air Medal he had won and the words of Rear Admiral Outlaw. Then he smiled.

"You know, Dad," he said, grinning, "I'm a little bit proud of myself."

A NAVY FLYER'S CREED

I am a United States Navy Flyer.

My countrymen built the best airplane in the world and entrusted it to me. They trained me to fly it. I will use it to the absolute limit of my power.

With my fellow pilots, air crews, and deck crew my plane and I will do anything necessary to carry out our tremendous responsibilities. I will aways remember we are part of an unbeatable combat team—the United States Navy. When the going is fast and rough, I will not falter. I will be uncompromising in every blow I strike. I will be humble in victory.

I am a United States Navy flyer. I have dedicated myself to my country, with its many millions of all races, colors, and creeds. They and their ways of life are worthy of my greatest protective effort.

I ask the help of God in making that effort great enough.

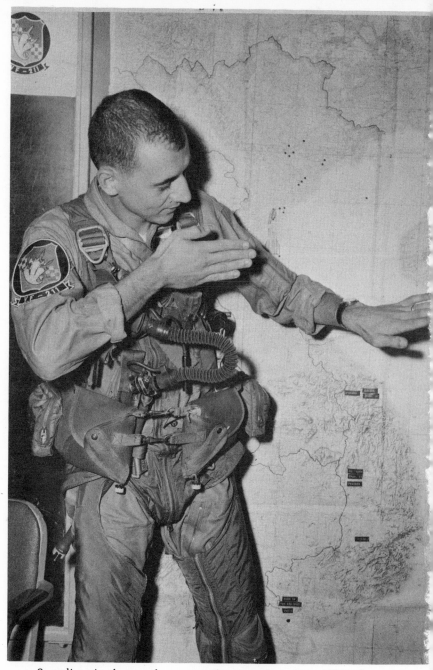

Standing in front of a map of target locations, Phil shows how he took his plane in on a bridge-destroying mission